From Broken Pieces
to a Full Basket

cc

FROM
BROKEN
PIECES
TO A
FULL BASKET

The Positive Side of Failure

Cheryl M. Smith

CHRISTIAN PUBLICATIONS
Camp Hill, Pennsylvania

Christian Publications
3825 Hartzdale Drive, Camp Hill, PA 17011

The mark of ✝ *vibrant faith*

ISBN: 0-87509-531-3
LOC Catalog Card Number: 93-70745
© 1993 by Christian Publications
All rights reserved
Printed in the United States of America

93 94 95 96 97   5 4 3 2 1

Cover Design: Step One Design

Acknowledgments

We all live and work in a web of relationships — friends, family and acquaintances that are important to us. Our lives are the products of such webs. In the same way, neither is this book the product of one solitary effort. Rather, it is a team product of faith and sacrifice on the part of many among whom are the following:

Jackie McCoy—it was Jackie's ministry in counseling that God used to inscribe on my life some of the concepts shared with you in this text.

Mary Webb—Mary has tirelessly proofread these pages, prayed and shared my vision of ministry to ministry wives with me.

Scott Smith—my husband, who always supports and encourages me to follow God's leading, and has especially done so in the writing of this book.

Doug and Betty Black—my parents, who not only encouraged me repeatedly, but have also provided the technology to finish the job.

Ray Rasmussen—for his help in preparing the final manuscript for the publishers.

To these folks, and others not mentioned, I am gratefully indebted.

Dedication

This book is dedicated to my sisters in ministry.

Contents

Preface

THREE TIGHTLY BUNDLED FIGURES walked slowly along the highway beneath a slate-gray January sky. The cold nipped their cheeks and the tips of their noses. But they didn't seem to mind. They were intent on winning the aluminum can contest the children's Sunday school had promoted to raise money for a missions project. So much so, that Carrie and Kelly had talked me into spending Saturday morning with them collecting cans along the highway outside of town.

"I see one!" Carrie exclaimed, rushing forward to reclaim a forsaken beer can from the weeds. With a rustle and a clank, the empty can fell into her bag along with the others. As we walked, clinking and clanking, our conversation evaporated into the frosty air around us.

"What does a pasture's wife do?" Kelly asked. I smiled at her simple confusion of terms. I knew Kelly was struggling to picture me out in a field somewhere. But in spite of her terminology, her question really echoes a common confusion regarding ministry wives. After all, we know what the pastor's usual role in church life is. But how should we regard the pastor's wife? Can she be befriended? What should the church expect from her in service? How does she handle the stresses of everyday life — of ministry life?

From Broken Pieces to a Full Basket: The Positive Side of Failure was originally submitted to the publisher as a manuscript entitled *Confessions of a Pastor's Wife*. The publisher thought the book had many valuable lessons on success and failure for Christian women from all walks of life who have experienced similar struggles. Therefore, the new title based upon the biblical lesson of how Jesus Christ was able to feed the multitudes in John 6:1–13 reflects what I hope will be the result of my personal quest to define success and failure. The Lord was more than able to take the broken pieces in my life and use them to my benefit as well as His glory. It is my prayer that you might grow deeper in your walk with Jesus Christ because of the insights in success and failure presented here.

In the pages ahead I share some of my difficulties, my heartaches and joys in ministry and some of the lessons that God has taught me that I believe are common to Christian women everywhere, particularly those who serve in some sort of ministry. You will certainly get a glimpse of the life of a pastor's wife from reading this book, too, and I'm sure you will find that we are not all that different—you and I.

What does God expect from us in the roles He's given us? What should we expect from ourselves? How much should we listen to the advice or criticism of others? I've attempted to answer these and other questions in the pages ahead.

And if you are a ministry wife, I hope above all, that my honesty will strengthen you to remain faithful in the unique calling God has given you. While many pastors' wives have wonderful ministry experiences, not everyone makes the adjustments easily. Oh, what I would have given for some honest survival stories our first years in ministry when I was struggling so! Dear sister, if you find yourself feeling less than successful in this ministry business, take heart. This book is especially for you.

One may assume because of my hardships in this mountain pastorate I would never desire to return to the community described here. Amazingly, just the opposite is true. Shared trials have a way of forging bonds of love between people. Those described here are my brothers and sisters in Christ, and I love them dearly. Therefore, although the incidents related from my personal life are true, the names of individuals involved have been changed to prevent any unintentional embarrassment.

I believe Jesus intends for each of us to live a successful, satisfying life. It is my prayer that *From Broken Pieces to a Full Basket* will be both an inspiration and a channel to making this discovery your own personal testimony as well.

Chapter One

Failure—Everybody's Doing It

I HAD RECEIVED AN ICY GREETING from Ginna when I spoke to her Monday morning. Vainly I tried to lighten our encounter with a little conversation.

"I've been thinking about starting a women's Bible study this fall. Do you think that is something you'd be interested in?" I queried.

"I don't know," she said stiffly. "I'm not sure I'll be here in the fall."

Ginna went on to say that she was thinking of leaving our church to attend elsewhere. She hinted that others were planning to do the same. When I inquired as to why she was leaving, she wouldn't say; just that it wasn't my husband's ministry that was at fault.

I was surprised and concerned. Ginna had attended the church for a long time. She must be pretty upset to consider leaving. Had I inadvertently done anything to offend her? I wasn't aware of anything, but I wanted to be sure. The next morning I dialed her number and asked.

"It's of the Lord that you've called," she said. "I guess I had better tell you the truth in love before someone else does. It's not your husband—it's you! Everyone is leaving the church because of you." Then she proceeded to tell me how I had failed to meet her (and others') expectations for a pastor's wife.

Failure—it hits us all, doesn't it? It is not always as blunt as this experience. But then we don't usually need someone to tell us when we've blown it royally, do we?

But what really is failure? What is success? What does God expect from us? What should we expect from ourselves? How much should we listen to the advice or criticism of others? And is success really available to everyone—or for just the lucky few?

As I was writing this book I occasionally asked people, "How would you describe a successful person?" As you can imagine, the answers were as varied as the people I spoke with:

"Energetic."
"He prospers in every area of life."
"Reliable and willing to accomplish a task."
"Happy with what he's doing."
"Drive, ambition and personality."

I wasn't surprised. As a pastor's wife in a small church in western Washington, my answers for many years would have been much the same. You see we all know (or think we know) what standards we must reach to feel successful. Just how many of us realize those dreams is yet another question. But one experience is common to us all—failure. Great or small, the pain of disillusionment has touched every life at one time or another. Yet remarkable as it seems, God will transform even tragedy into personal victory for those with a humble heart attitude.

Nowhere is this better illustrated than in two Old Testament kingly biographies listed back-to-back in First and Second Samuel. But before we consider their stories, let's step back even farther into history to the events that set the stage for the anointing of Israel's first king.

King Saul

It's a comfort to me that whenever God calls us to a task, He equips us to succeed. And such was the case with Saul. Saul was a tall and handsome man. The Bible says he was taller and more handsome than anyone else in the nation. Not only did he have a regal bearing, but he was clearly God's choice as well. First Samuel 9:17 says "When Samuel caught sight of Saul, the LORD said to him, 'This is the man I spoke to you about; he will govern my people.' " Chapter 10 goes on to record an experience where Saul is filled with the Holy Spirit (10:6-7). Saul had it all—the looks, the anointing of God and God's empowering as well. How could he go wrong?

But fail is just what Saul did. Chapter 13 tells the story of one of Israel's many skirmishes with their militant neighbors, the Philistines. This time, as they met for battle, Israel was encamped within sight of the Philistine forces. As they gazed across the open space between them, Israel was stunned at the military strength of the Philistines. The Bible tells us the Philistines had 30,000 chariots and 6,000 horsemen ready for battle! The other forces were so numerous that they were impossible to estimate. The Bible simply describes them "as numerous as the sand on the seashore" (13:5)! Who wouldn't have second thoughts before an army like that?

Now it had been agreed that Samuel (the high priest) would arrive before battle to offer a sacrifice. King Saul was to await Samuel's arrival for this ceremony before leading his men into battle. To his credit, Saul waited seven days. During those seven days the psychological impact of the amassing Philistine forces began to take it's toll on Saul's troops. Many deserted and fled. The ones who remained were trembling in their sandals. As Saul waited and watched the demoralizing of his men, the temptation was strong to stop waiting and take matters into his own hands.

Finally he felt he could wait no longer. Impulsively, Saul took Samuel's place and performed the sacrifice.

Patience is a great virtue. (Perhaps that is why it takes an entire lifetime to cultivate it.) Patience is a virtue because it always raises the issue of dependence. It asks us whether we are willing to wait upon God, or whether we will again rely on our own abilities in the circumstances confronting us. As Saul wrestled with this issue, he decided to forsake God and handle the situation himself. The consequences of his decision would be devastating.

As soon as Saul had finished offering the sacrifices, Samuel arrived. "What have you done?" Samuel asked Saul (13:11). Saul responded with a perfect rationalization. In effect, he told Samuel that he was unaware of the circumstances. The people were scared and deserting; something had to be done. "So [Saul] felt compelled to offer the burnt offering" (13:12).

We are so quick to rationalize our wrongs, aren't we? "But God, you just don't understand. . . . I had no choice! . . . It's really not that big a thing, God. Besides, a lot of people do it." But rationalizing to protect our own ego is simply the defense of pride, not humility.

Pride—that original sin that caused Satan to fall from the heights of heaven. Pride—that voice that suggested to Eve that she could be like God if she would only seize the opportunity. God hates pride. Proverbs 15:25 warns, "The LORD tears down the proud man's house. . . ." And 16:5 says: "The LORD detests all the proud of heart. Be sure of this: They will not go unpunished." So it would be with Saul.

Disobedience springs directly from the "pride of life" (1 John 2:16), that inner motivation that tempts us to try and usurp God on the throne of our lives. God hates pride and the disobedience that goes with it. No matter how we fool ourselves and others with our intricate lies, blaming and rationalizations, we will never fool God. Grudging, incomplete obedience is still, in the end, simple rebellion.

But God is a loving Sovereign to those that are His. In Jeremiah 31:3 He says, "I have loved you with an everlasting love." First John 4:8 describes God's very nature as being that of love ("God is love"). Because of His love, God hates to punish us. Yet because God is our Heavenly Father, He knows that, undisciplined, we will wreck our lives and incur suffering beyond description. That sin always bears consequences is, for the unsaved, God's justice. For the saved, consequences are the spanking stick of love. Will there be scars? Sometimes. But the only scars our Savior leaves in the lives of His children remain to remind us of His deliverance and keep us from destruction. The amazing truth of failure in the Christian experience is that it can always be turned into success if we will but humble ourselves under the discipline of God!

I remember the afternoon Vicki came to visit. She sat at my kitchen table and talked brokenly with tears streaming down her cheeks. Vicki's first marriage was a brutal experience that ended in divorce and left her with three children and little else. She found new life and hope in a relationship with Jesus Christ. Since I had known her, she had also remarried. This time her husband was a warm and loving Christian man. Life was improving for her, but the battles for visitation rights with her ex-husband left her wounded and crushed repeatedly. This day she asked simply, "When does it end, Cheryl? When does it ever end?" As I put my arms around her, I wished I had the answer. Today. Tomorrow. Next week or year.

But sometimes it simply takes time, years perhaps, for the sting of our failures to cease. These are the times when we can rediscover Christ's sufficiency for us. That same sufficiency we knew so deeply as we fell humbly to our knees in our first crisis. Above and beyond all else, Christ wants us to realize that He is our all; our very life. When we have this integrated into our lives, little else around us will matter. The scars may remain, but the sting will be gone.

Let's look at another kingly biography in light of success and failure.

King David

David—chosen of God, a handsome man, filled with the Holy Spirit, musically gifted, a mighty warrior and, as he matured, wise in his speech. He had all he needed to be a successful ruler over Israel. And successful he indeed was, but not so much because he avoided failure. Rather, David experienced success because he practiced a humble heart attitude.

David's military acumen brought him fame and fortune. He enlarged Israel's holdings, amassed an incredible fortune, developed a formidable army and had all the wives he could want. One would think so much would eventually be enough. But apparently this was not the case. One evening as David strolled in the cool of the evening on the palace roof, he looked down upon the city and noticed a woman bathing. Temptation turned to lust, and David sent and had the woman, Bathsheba, brought to the palace where he had sexual relations with her. It is unclear how long their adulterous relationship continued. Bathsheba's husband, Uriah, was in the army and away at war, so the relationship could have continued for some time. But finally came the message that all secret lovers dread—Bathsheba was expecting.

David quickly formed a cover-up scheme. He had Uriah brought home on leave. David expected the weary soldier to arrive home eager to enjoy relations with his wife. Then when news of the coming baby reached him, Uriah would think the child was his own.

A great plan. There was only one problem. It didn't work! Uriah didn't go home! As night fell, he was found, instead, sleeping at the door of the king's house with the other servants. Uriah felt it was unfair to his men for him to enjoy the comforts of home while they were still away at war. Even when David got him drunk the following night, Uriah did not return home.

Finally David wrote some grim orders: "Put Uriah in the front line where the fighting is fiercest. Then withdraw from him so he will be struck down and die" (2 Samuel 11:15). He summoned Uriah, and sent him back to the battle carrying orders for his own death. Now the hands that had been stained with illicit passion were stained in blood as well. David was both adulterer and murderer.

David's final cover-up plan seemed to work. Uriah became a supposed casualty of war. Bathsheba went through the usual span allotted for mourning and then was brought by David to the palace to become his wife and give birth to their son. No doubt, they felt they had gotten away with it. And if anyone did secretly question their relationship, they would certainly not be so bold as to confront the king about it. Uriah was dead. What did it matter now that the son born by his wife was in fact David's child and not Uriah's?

But it mattered to God. God had seen David's lust, adultery and cold-blooded murder scheme. And He sent a prophet to tell David so.

Nathan must have been a man of incredible

courage, totally committed to God's leading in his life. How else can you explain his fulfilling a mission that involved telling Israel's foremost warrior-king that the sin he had worked so hard to cover over was known to God, and that he would be disciplined for his failure? I certainly wouldn't have wanted to stand in Nathan's shoes! Yet this is just what Nathan did. He asked David to judge a story about two men. One was a wealthy man who had many flocks of sheep. The other was a poor man who owned only one lamb and loved it like a family pet. Yet when the wealthy man entertained guests, he went and stole the poor man's lamb, and served it to his guests, rather than providing a meal from his own ample flocks.

The Bible says that when Nathan finished the story, David became furious. "As surely as the LORD lives," he thundered, "the man who did this deserves to die! He must pay for that lamb four times over, because he did such a thing and had no pity" (12:5-6).

Nathan's answer to David was concise and dramatic: "You are the man!" (12:7).

He then went on to remind David of all that God had given him: "And if all this had been too little, I would have given you even more" (12:8). Then the prophet asked, "Why did you despise the word of the LORD by doing what is evil in His eyes?" (12:9). He listed in detail the events David thought were hidden and almost forgotten.

Then Nathan began to list the consequences David's failure would cost him. They would be four-fold, just as David gave verdict that the poor man whose lamb was stolen should be reimbursed four-fold. First, "The sword will never depart from your house, because you despised me and took the wife of Uriah the Hittite to be your own" (12:10). Second, "Out of your own household I [God] am going to bring calamity upon you" (12:11). Third, "Before your very eyes I will take your wives and give them to one who is close to you, and he will lie with your wives in broad daylight" (12:12). And last, "Because by doing this you have made the enemies of the LORD show utter contempt, the son born to you will die" (12:14).

What was David's response? "Then David said to Nathan, 'I have sinned against the LORD' " (12:13). Psalm 51 records David's confession in greater detail. He openly admits his sin (51:4), asks for God's forgiveness and cleansing (51:7), and then asks that God restore him spiritually (51:10-17) and bless Israel (51:18-19). Unlike Saul and his proud rationalizations, David humbly repented and accepted God's discipline.

Sin's Consequences

Both Saul and David bore the consequences of their sin. Yet no two men's life experiences were ever more different. Because of Saul's failure to obey, God removed the right to rule from Saul's lineage. Saul, himself, would finish his reign on the throne of Israel, but his son would never succeed him (1 Samuel 13:13-14; 15:26-28). Yet unlike David, Saul hardened his heart against God's discipline. Rather than repent and enjoy the life God had granted him, Saul's life became an obsessive, bitter, downward spiral that ended in defeat and despair. Grasping for a future he could not have, he lost the successful life experience God intended to give him.

Although Saul voiced repentance at various times, it was never humility of any depth. Finally, facing what was to be his last battle, Saul realized the depths of despair to which his pride had plummeted him. As he inquired of the Lord for guidance in the battle before him, "the Lord did not answer him" (1 Samuel 28:6). Yet instead of humbly doing a personal spiritual inventory before the Lord, Saul disguised himself and went to visit a medium. Earlier in his reign Saul had purged Israel of those dealing in the occult (28:3). The penalty for anyone dabbling in such areas was death. So the medium was clearly hesitant when disguised King Saul asked her to summon Samuel from the dead. Saul's response again indicates how low Saul had sunk. For he pledged to protect her and sealed the vow in God's own name! When Samuel was summoned from the dead, Saul's final words echo the dregs of a life of failure.

"Why have you disturbed me by bringing me up?" Samuel asked Saul. " 'I am in great distress,' Saul said. 'The Philistines are fighting against me, and God has turned away from me. He no longer answers me, either by prophets or by dreams. So I have called on you to tell me what to do.' Samuel said, 'Why do you consult me, now that the LORD has turned away from you and become your enemy?' " (28:15-16).

Distressed and forsaken, Saul died in battle the following day. His entire reign was a mere shadow of what could have been.

David, on the other hand, experienced all the heartache that the prophet Nathan foretold. Soon after Nathan's visit the baby born to David and Bathsheba died (2 Samuel 12:15-23). Later David's son, Absalom murdered his half brother Amnon (13:24-29). In time Absalom also stole the kingdom away from David and sent him fleeing in shame to exile (15:1-37). While David was in exile, Absalom pitched a tent on the palace roof and publicly had sexual relations with all of David's wives (16:21-22). Eventually, this son, too, died even against David's strict orders (18:5, 9-15). These surely were bitter consequences. But rather than become hardened, David humbly accepted God's chastening. The result is echoed in his last song.

"When one rules over men in righteousness,
    when he rules in the fear of God,
he is like the light of morning at sunrise
    on a cloudless morning,
like the brightness after rain
    that brings the grass from the earth."

Is not my house right with God?
    Has he not made with me an everlasting
      covenant,
    arranged and secured in every part?
Will he not bring to fruition my salvation
    and grant me my every desire? (23:3-5)

Failure Doesn't Have to Be Final

How different from the words of King Saul—"I am in great distress . . . and God has turned away from me" (1 Samuel 28:15). David was a man who ended a life pockmarked by failure, with a deep sense of satisfaction, trust and love for God. The difference, I believe, was not in the degree of failure, but in the response to it.

How did I handle my own failure that day Ginna criticized me? I'd like to report that I handled her honesty with grace and humility. But that wasn't the case. Instead, I raged in hurt and anger behind the closed doors of the parsonage.

"Can you believe it?" I complained to my husband. "With the new baby, it's all I can do to get the basics done right now. And she has the gall to criticize me for not being involved enough in church life. I'll bet she never accomplished half of what I do when her children were this size!"

Eventually I was able to admit the truth in some of the criticisms Ginna leveled against me. And I had to admit that my own spirit had been likewise critical of others in the congregation. In part, I was reaping the bitter harvest of my own harsh attitudes. My criticisms were unspoken to all but my husband, but God had seen my arrogance. And it apparently showed on the outside as well.

Ginna's words hurt me badly. My husband later spoke with her and she admitted where she was wrong. Like all of us at times, Ginna had given verdict without all the facts.

For my part, I came out of the experience wounded, but humbler. I confessed my wrong before God. I looked beyond Ginna's words to try and gather her perspective. And in time I was able to put my arms around her and tell her I loved her. I meant it, too. The divisions of the past were gone. And the lessons I learned about success and failure have proved invaluable.

God told Paul, "My grace is sufficient for you, for

my power is made perfect in weakness" (2 Corinthians 12:9). God longs to take our failures and turn them into His glorifying successes. Failure is not the end. For Christians just the opposite may be true. A point of weakness may be the door to a glorious beginning. The future hinges on a humble heart attitude.

MAKING IT YOURS

1. How would you rate yourself as a "successful" person? (1 being the lowest value; 10 being the highest value)

2. At what value point would you begin to apply the term "failure"?

3. In what areas of life do you consider "success" to be most important? (ex. career, marriage, education, etc.)

4. God never calls us to a role without providing the enabling to fill it (Ephesians 2:10; Philippians 2:13). What are some roles God has given you? (ex. teacher, wife, etc.)

5. How has God enabled you to fill those roles?

6. King Saul and King David each responded to failure and its consequences differently. King Saul was proud and defensive. King David humbly confessed his sin, sought forgiveness and accepted sin's consequences. Which model would you choose for your life and why?

7. How can failure be a new beginning and not a bitter end? What attitude is key to such a change?

Chapter Two

How's Your Resumé?

IT HAD BEEN A WONDERFUL DINNER. The fellowship with other pastors and their wives was rich and
full of laughter as always. Yet as the emcee inventoried
the churches represented at our meeting, I secretly
wished that somehow I could crawl under the table
and disappear. Name after name was called. Each
church responded, as pastoral staff and board members stood proudly to identify themselves. Inwardly I
cringed and hoped we'd be forgotten.

Our ministry had been a struggle from the day
we accepted the small pastorate in western
Washington. It wasn't that we hadn't tried. My
husband and I had been over the "why doesn't it
grow?" problem from every angle. Yet we had not
seen definite results. Results that were measurable,
that is. The fact that only one of our governing
board had been able to attend this function with
us seemed to be another testimony of our failure.

But was it really a failure? Can success always be measured in numbers? After all Isaiah described Christ's resumé in less than glowing terms:

> He grew up before him like a tender shoot,
>   and like a root out of dry ground.
> He had no beauty or majesty to attract us to
>   him,
>   nothing in his appearance that we should
>   desire him.
> He was despised and rejected by men,
>   a man of sorrows, and familiar with suffering.
> Like one from whom men hide their faces
>   he was despised, and we esteemed him not.
>   (Isaiah 53:2-3)

This seems an unlikely resumé for the Son of God, doesn't it? But the fact is that God doesn't judge success and failure as we do. First Corinthians 1:27 says that "God chose the foolish things of the world to shame the wise." So what really is success? How does one define it, and how can we be sure that definition is correct?

The Pharisees

The Pharisees were a select religious club. In fact, their title comes from a Hebrew word meaning "separated ones." The pride they took in meticulously following the Law and Judaic tradition was also usually accompanied by an arrogant, self-righteous attitude toward others not as religious as themselves.

In many ways they were not unlike many of the clubs, political groups or professional associations that exist in our society today. We have many of them. In fact, from the cradle to the grave we are continually comparing, evaluating and defining our places in society. Not that social definition is all wrong. But when such thinking becomes the basis of measuring self worth, the Bible has some strong challenges for Christians.

The Pharisees took great pride in their ancestry. They were Jews, the chosen people of God. Because of God's promise to Abraham, they assumed they had an automatic position of righteousness. Jesus rebuked their assumptions in Matthew 3:8-9:

> Produce fruit in keeping with repentance. And do not think you can say to yourselves, "We have Abraham as our father." I tell you that out of these stones God can raise up children for Abraham.

Heritage, no matter how outstanding, is never the basis for judging success as far as God is concerned. We may have a justifiable pride in our ethnic roots, an imposing ancestry or religious background, but ultimately each man will himself have to give account before God. No lineage, no matter how impressive, will matter there.

Their Jewish identity was not the Pharisees' only claim to success, however. More than their "Jewishness," the Pharisees looked to their meticulous observance of the Law as the basis for their assumption of superiority. Again Jesus exposed their error. In Matthew 6:2-16 Jesus mentioned three areas of religiousness that the Pharisees were prone to flaunt: their giving, their ability to pray in public and their religious lifestyle as seen both in their public prayers and fasting. Jesus said instead that true worship is a private affair. Giving, prayer and any special lifestyle God calls us to are to be lived first and foremost before God. The Pharisees, as Jesus observed in Luke 16:15, lived their lives primarily for the approval of others.

It's an easy trap to fall into—judging one another's spiritual success by the religious trappings hanging about our lives. How quickly we assume that the greatest giver at church should also be given a seat on the governing board. How many of us struggle with untrue feelings of spiritual inferiority when we listen to someone's flowing prayer full of impressive words and religious phrases? A talented speaker or teacher is placed on a mental pedestal of spirituality. No wonder we are so shocked when they turn out to be less than what we imagined.

Material Possessions

If success can't be defined by our outward spirituality, what about measuring it by our assets or annual income? After all don't we usually assume the driver of a new BMW is more successful than someone behind the wheel of a dilapidated pickup truck? One thing's for sure; he'll probably pay more for car insurance! But does the prestige the world attributes to possessions and income truly measure success in God's eyes?

In Luke 12 Jesus tells a parable about possessions. It seems there was a rich farmer who had done well for himself. In fact, he had done so well that he needed to build additional barns to hold all his harvest. After he did that, he planned to take life easy and enjoy his retirement. Up to this point in the story Jesus does not fault the farmer. He has worked hard and earned his reward of ease. What Jesus does fault him for is that he hasn't worked equally as hard to prepare for eternity (12:20). In effect, Jesus says that material possessions are transient and matter little in comparison to our investment in eternal things.

The world will sell you just the opposite line if it can. But as Jesus asked in Matthew 16:26, "What good will it be for a man if he gains the whole world, yet forfeits his soul? Or what can a man give in exchange for his soul?" No, possessions can never be the measure of success.

What then is the standard by which we can measure success? Consider these three men: John the Baptist, Jesus and the Apostle Paul. They could all be considered failures by worldly standards. Each lived a life of poverty and self-sacrifice. Each died a martyr's death and left behind only a handful of disciples. Yet, in spite of continual criticism and trials, each experienced a profound sense of fulfillment and accomplishment. Their lives give testimony to the true basis for measuring success.

John the Baptist

After Jesus arrived on the scene, attendance at John's baptisms began declining. To John's disciples, it hardly seemed fair. After all, it was John's ministry that had been established first. And it was John who baptized Jesus, validating His ministry. John's disciples were confused and perhaps a little jealous. They came to John with their observation. "Rabbi, that man who was with you on the other side of the Jordan—the one you testified about—well, he is baptizing, and everyone is going to him" (John 3:26).

John's answer is classic. "A man can receive only what is given him from heaven" (3:27). Did you get that? Success comes from God! We are only recipients, nothing more. Hebrews 3:4 says, "For every house is built by someone, but God is the builder of everything."

What does this mean? It means that God is ultimately the giver of success. It means that you can do everything right and never see measurable results. It means you may not be the failure that you thought you were. Not every successful ministry grows. Not every responsible employee gets ahead. Not every zealous Christian is perfectly understood. But that's okay. Failing before others is not necessarily failure before God.

But how did John handle the reality of a shrinking ministry? He handled it by knowing his role and being satisfied in it. He replies: "I am not the Christ but am sent ahead of him" (John 3:28).

Isn't this an amazing statement? The world would have us believe just the opposite is true—I must increase, you must decrease! We're always competing. We're always striving to do one better; to push the other guy aside and claw our way to the top. Then John comes along and says it isn't necessary. The only truly important thing is to be faithful and satisfied in our God-given roles.

I used to wonder how my husband could attend the area pastors' functions for our denomination. He hardly ever missed. Yet our ministry was going so poorly I would have been embarrassed to go. One day I asked him, "How can you stand to go to those pastors' meetings? Doesn't it just tear you up inside to hear how everyone else's ministry is going so well, while you have so little to share?"

I'll never forget my husband's answer. "Honey," he said tenderly, "those men love us. They know what a difficult ministry this is, and they pray for us. I'm just excited about hearing what God is doing in other places, as well."

Do you struggle with jealousy? Does your heart burn with anger over something you perceive as unfair in your life? Then step back in time with John the Baptist. Ask God to help you be content in the role He's entrusted to you. After all, being faithful in a role that offers few outward perks is much tougher than one where results flow easily.

Jesus

The private prayer of Christ on behalf of His followers is found in John 17. In it He reveals an interesting truth relating to our search to define success. Jesus says to the Father, "I have brought you glory on earth by completing the work you gave me to do" (17:4). This truth was brought into focus again when Christ hung on a cross dying under the searing Mediterranean sun. During His crucifixion, He had raised Himself on tortured limbs for various exclamations. But it was His last cry that should be carefully considered, for it was at that last moment of life Christ cried out, "It is finished" (19:30). Jesus had done the job the Father had sent Him to do. His cry was not simply a statement of fact, but a cry of exultation; a statement of simple success—faithfulness.

We spent four years in that difficult ministry in western Washington. For three of those years, the church hardly grew. The same faces showed up from week to week. Sometimes a new face would replace an old one. But the church never seemed to thrive, no matter what we did. In fact, it often seemed more a case of resuscitation than a celebration of new life in Christ!

Finally, we began an evangelistic visitation ministry. Those outside the church began to hear and receive the gospel. Over the next four months our church nearly doubled in attendance. We were thrilled! Ironically, God had also opened the door to a new ministry opportunity. Now we tearfully struggled over the same move we hungered for a year earlier. Yet, in our hearts, we knew our ministry there was coming to an end.

Moving day wasn't easy. There were regrets, and there were tears. Yet underneath the heartache was a silent exultation similar to Christ's triumphant cry. It was a rejoicing not based on church growth or the new opportunities ahead, but a rejoicing in knowing we had finished a task. By God's grace we'd stayed through the tough years. And now, by that same grace, we were moving on. Faithfulness. It's so simple, yet so hard. But truly this is the bottom line on success before God.

Apostle Paul

So if God is the Judge of success, what do we do with the opinions of others? Do we listen to their criticisms or praise, or do we simply write them off?

Paul struggled with criticism. (So if you've been criticized unfairly recently, take heart and consider yourself in good company.) It seems that some of the Corinthians felt Paul simply didn't match up with his writings or with other speakers they had heard. How did he handle their accusations? He handled them by refusing to play the comparison game. Paul knew we each have our own unique role in God's kingdom. If we are going to boast, we should boast only in fulfilling that which God has called us to do. As the Bible says, " 'Let him who boasts boast in the Lord.' For it is not the man who commends himself who is approved, but the man whom the Lord commends" (2 Corinthians 10:17-18).

The Comparison Game

This truth hit home in my life early in our first pastorate. True to my perfectionist nature, I was very intent on meeting the church's expectations and fulfilling my role as the pastor's wife. This meant that I had a mental checklist against which I daily measured my performance. Included on my list of "things a good pastor's wife does" were:

- attends all church functions
- sets the example in hospitality
- visits church members with her husband
- contributes her talents in music, teaching, etc.
- assumes (gladly), and executes (competently) various leadership roles, such as women's functions, Sunday school, etc.
- stays on top of things both spiritually and emotionally . . .

I'll conclude my list there. Amazingly there were still many more qualifications I was trying to meet. I'm sure you get the idea. But no one can always meet everyone's expectations, and there was certainly no way I could live up to my own. As the mother of a toddler who was soon confronted with the arrival of another infant, my reality called for goals that had to do with simply making it through the day! To realize the expectations I had set for myself, I needed a clone—one me to stay at home and deal with the day to day, another to do all the work of the "ministry."

The result of this pressure was that my life was literally torn apart! Instead of maintaining emotional and spiritual control, I began a downward spiral into the dark abyss of clinical depression. And in my despair, I struggled with an overwhelming sense of failure, alienation and tremendous anger toward God. After all, He had called me here to be a pastor's wife and now my entire world was falling apart!

It was about this time that I came across First Corinthians 4:3-5:

> I care very little if I am judged by you or by any human court; indeed, I do not even judge myself. My conscience is clear, but that does not make me innocent. It is the Lord who judges me. Therefore judge nothing before the appointed time; wait till the Lord comes. He will bring to light what is hidden in darkness and will expose the motives of men's hearts. At that time each will receive his praise from God.

I want you to notice several things from this passage. First, it is truly a small thing what other people think of us. We should be humble enough to consider their criticisms or praise. If there is merit in it, receive it. Yet, all in all, the opinions of others matter little to God. Second, Paul doesn't even judge himself as a success or failure and we shouldn't either. It is often true we can be our own worst critics. To do so is folly. Only God knows in full all that He hopes for us to accomplish. The reality is that we may be doing better than we think! Third, it is important what God thinks of us! Success is being found faithful in doing the jobs we've been given.

And last, God will judge us not only on our performance, but by the motives of our hearts. This is a great anchor of hope and joy to me. This means that when our best intentions go awry, when our greatest plans fall flat and when our critics are at our heels, God knows the motives of our hearts and will judge intentions as well as performance. In love He surrounds us in a mighty embrace and says, "It's all right. I know you meant things to turn out differently. Your heart is right and that's the root of faithfulness. Well done, good and faithful servant."

Are you facing a tough assignment? Perhaps, like the church described here, you are dealing with a ministry that seems fruitless, and you are tempted to quit and walk away. Perhaps you are thinking about abandoning a difficult marriage, job or relationship. Let me encourage you to hang in there. Faithfulness may not always bring results we can see and measure, but it is the yardstick by which God measures all believers. What is faithfulness? It is staying until your job is done. It is staying until your cry can become one with Christ's, "It is finished!"— that's success!

MAKING IT YOURS

1. What are some ways people commonly judge success?

2. What standards of comparison did the Pharisees use to distinguish the spiritually successful? (Matthew 3:7-9; 6:1-18)

3. What does Jesus teach us about making financial or material gain the method of measuring success? (Matthew 6:19-24; Luke 12:15-21)

4. Where did John the Baptist say success comes from? (John 3:27)

5. Why wasn't John jealous of Jesus' ministry? (John 3:22-30)

6. What did Jesus mean when He cried, "It is finished!"? (John 17:4-8; 19:28-30)

7. What did Paul mean when he wrote that those who "compare themselves with themselves, they are not wise"? (2 Corinthians 10:10-18)

8. Read 1 Corinthians 4:3-5. What four principles for judging success does Paul refer to in this passage?

9. Which of these principles do you most need to apply to your life right now? Why?

Chapter Three

About Throwing That First Stone

I SAT IN THE LAST ROW OF CHURCH and struggled with my two restless preschoolers. Although our church did provide nursery care during the morning service, it was not available for the evening service. Now, as I struggled in vain to keep the children quiet and yet give my attention to the service, I began to wonder why I even bothered to come. I was unable to concentrate on the service, being terribly aware that my children were quickly becoming a distraction. To be honest, I felt more frustrated than blessed. Finally, as so often happened, I gave up, collected our things and left. Behind the closed doors of home, I gave myself up to tears.

It was wrestling experiences such as these that finally convinced me that I had two options. I could either stay home until my children could sit through church (with the exception of the morning service), or the children and I could attend elsewhere on Sunday and Wednesday nights, where nursery care was provided. Realizing I could not endure long in an environment of isolation and that my daughter needed social interaction with other children, my husband and I decided that I should attend these services in another church some distance away. We both knew that without emotional support and fellowship, our ministry in this community would be cut short. Perhaps with the friendships I would experience elsewhere I would in turn be greater strengthened to give of myself to our ministry.

This was a difficult decision. Attending part of the time elsewhere meant I struggled to feel a sense of belonging at either church. Yet, it seemed the best option open to our family at the time. It is not surprising that my actions were misunderstood by those in our own church. After all, I would have questioned such behavior myself, I suppose. What was hurtful was that I was judged before I was asked to explain.

One evening I tried attending our services again. And again the results were the same. I left for home shortly after the service began, in frustration and despair. I had no sooner arrived at home than there was a knock at the door. I opened it and there stood a woman from church. I was upset and really not ready for a visitor and told her so; but she insisted she needed to talk with me. If I had known the nature of her visit, I would probably never have allowed her in. For she sat next to me on the couch and proceeded to list all the ways I was failing as a pastor's wife. A good part of her criticism stemmed from my decision to attend this other fellowship. It was clear she had simply stopped by to deliver a verbal stoning.

At first I tried to explain my actions. But it soon became obvious that she had come intent on hearing a confession and was staying until she heard one. So I eventually confessed to her charges. Not that I was repentant, mind you. Instead, my heart was raging in rebellion. But I wanted—I needed—the conversation to end. She concluded her visit by praying that I would have a change of heart regarding ministry life.

It was a prayer that found an immediate answer. But certainly not the answer she had intended. For never had I felt more defeated as a ministry wife than at that moment. I was both angry and hurt. I was angered by her arrogant judgment, hurt by her lack of understanding. I was bitter over her insensitivity. And her condescending prayer repulsed me. How quickly she had forgotten the demanding days when her own children were preschoolers. How little she cared to understand the added pressures of ministry under which I labored.

And if the damage of this evening weren't painful enough, I would soon discover this woman had sowed these same accusations in the hearts of others as well. Ginna was one that would be drawn into this gossip. And when Ginna talked with me later, she made it clear that others were involved as well. The "others" remained nameless, of course. And the result, personally, was a tremendous sense of insecurity and isolation.

Now every parishioner became a suspected critic.

Feelings of worthlessness and rejection enveloped me each time I stepped into a Sunday service. "No one wants you here," Satan would whisper. "You're no good for your husband. He'd be better off without you. Take the kids and leave while you are young enough to start over." Repeatedly these and other such thoughts rankled my mind. Often my only defense was in knowing that, as incompetent as I may have seemed to some, I had not yet surrendered the fight. "At least I've stayed." I argued mentally. "That's more than many would have done. Faithfulness—that's got to count for something!"

I've learned since then that such secretive and critical attacks against a ministry family are not at all uncommon. I'm sure if this situation were to happen again, I wouldn't take it nearly so personally. But this experience was truly a baptism by fire that caught me unawares.

It's so easy to judge what we don't understand. To understand another takes time and compassion. Often it means humbly realizing that we all have the potential for any sin within ourselves. We lack only the circumstances to propel us in that direction. Judgment is easier. It appeals more to our ego. But it is only as we lay aside our judgmental attitudes and realize our common vulnerability to failure, that we are drawn closer to one another in compassion and humility.

In the previous lesson we examined the Pharisees' reputation for self-righteousness. Obviously they were wrong in living to hear the praise of others. But were they so wrong in confronting those who had truly fallen into sin? When do we have the Christian right to confront? A confrontation with Jesus over the judging of a woman caught in the very act of adultery raises some interesting questions.

A Tricky Predicament

In this story (John 8:1-11) the Pharisees brought before Jesus a woman caught in an adulterous relationship. We aren't told what happened, if anything, to her partner. He was either not present or simply not identified. The Pharisees' goal was primarily to trap Jesus in a complex religious question. According to the Law, adultery was punishable by death (Leviticus 20:10). And since there was no doubt regarding this woman's sin, a verdict of death by stoning seemed inevitable. If Christ offered such a decision, He would discredit His ministry and reputation as the "friend of sinners." If He excused her, the Pharisees would have proof that Jesus was not upholding the Law. It did indeed seem an impossible situation.

But Jesus turned the tables. Stooping down before the onlookers and crowd of haughty Pharisees, Jesus began to write in the dust with His finger. We aren't told what He wrote; perhaps it was names, perhaps offenses. After a bit Jesus stood up and said simply, "If any one of you is without sin, let him be the first to throw a stone at her" (John 8:7).

One can almost hear the stones dropping, one by one, out of sweaty palms and back into the dirt. The one who was without sin was invited to throw the first stone; but no one is sinless. One by one the Pharisees realized that they were unqualified to act as executioners. They may have been religious men, but they were not perfectly righteous. Like everyone else—like this woman—they had their areas of vulnerability.

Only One was present who was sinless enough to cast a stone and He chose not to. After the Pharisees had left, Jesus straightened up and faced the accused woman. There was no lecture from Him on immorality. He uttered not even a mild reprimand. Instead Jesus simply asked:

> "Woman, where are they? Has no one condemned you?"
> "No one, sir," she said.
> "Then neither do I condemn you," Jesus declared. "Go now and leave your life of sin." (8:10-11)

Was it right of Jesus to let her off so lightly? Absolutely. You see Jesus' ministry was new and different from the legalism of the past. John 1:17 says, "For the law was given through Moses; grace and truth came through Jesus Christ." Jesus came to forgive; to initiate a relationship with God, not rupture it. Paul says that, after all, the Law was only "put in charge to lead us to Christ that we might be justified by faith" (Galatians 3:24). Justification with God—this was the central goal behind Christ's ministry and ultimately, His death. So as Jesus faced this woman and her sin, He became her Advocate. He defended her, offered her forgiveness, and charged her to "leave [her] life of sin" (John 8:11).

A New Ministry

Aren't you glad Jesus came in grace and truth? His whole focus is not judgment, but is, instead, to make the "poor" rich, to set the "prisoners" free, to give "sight to the blind" and restore the "oppressed" (Luke 4:18-19). Ephesians 2:1-3 reveals how lost we are without Christ. Without Him we are spiritually dead, buried beneath the condemning record of our sins. Worse yet our sins are simply evidence of a greater fault, that our very natures are Satanic and opposed to God. Without Christ we merit only God's wrath, not His forgiveness.

But the wonder is that God, "who is rich in mercy" (2:4), loved us. He sent Christ to die on our behalf, thereby paying the legal penalty of sin that God's justice required and offering us forgiveness and new life. Under His influence the things that once characterized our old way of life are replaced with reflections of God Himself (Galatians 5:19-23).

The Deception of Self-Righteousness
The only problem is that Satan doesn't surrender lives easily. First Peter 5:8 describes him as "Your enemy . . . a roaring lion looking for someone to devour." And Paul reminds the Corinthian Church that Satan is a great deceiver that even "masquerades as an angel of light" (2 Corinthians 11:14).

One such deception is that often we subtly begin to take credit for the life changes that the Holy Spirit has been making. And as we grow apart from grace in our self-righteous attitude, we become ready critics of others. Instead of "seeking to save the lost" (Luke 19:10, NASB), as Christ came to do, we begin to compare—to judge, and condemn or approve as we see fit. How quickly we forget that once we were separated from God's grace. Whether we realize it or not, we've allowed our pharisaical attitudes to separate us again from that grace. And this separation is to Satan's advantage.

A Lesson in Confrontation

After Jesus' death, Peter and some of the other disciples returned to their profession as fishermen. One morning following a fruitless night of fishing, Christ appeared on the shore.

> He called out to them, "Friends, haven't you any fish?"
> "No," they answered.
> He said, "Throw your net on the right side of the boat and you will find some."(John 21:5-6)

They cast their nets accordingly and the fish filled the nets to overflowing. Something clicked in Peter's mind. He recalled the memory of when he and Jesus first met, when Jesus filled the nets to overflowing and then proclaimed to Peter, "from now on you will catch men" (Luke 5:10b). "It is the Lord!" John cried to Peter (John 21:7). Immediately Peter was overboard swimming to shore to meet Jesus.

If I had been Jesus, I think I might have been tempted to write Peter off. After all Jesus had warned him repeatedly that he would be tempted to deny Jesus. And still Peter refused to take heed. Why waste any more time on someone who couldn't be trusted? But Jesus comes gently to us following our failures. He comes not in judgment, but reminding us of His love and our special relationship with Him. I wonder how often we fall short in likewise restoring others who have failed us? Do we come in a spirit of grace and tenderness, or is our manner harsh and rough? Galatians 6:1 says: "Brothers, if someone is caught in a sin, you who are spiritual should restore him gently. But watch yourself, or you also may be tempted."

And Paul urged the Corinthian church to reaffirm, forgive and comfort a Christian who had repented under church discipline. That there is a place for confrontation in our relationships, becomes clear as Jesus' dialogue with Peter continues. What also becomes clear is that godly confrontation is also tempered with love and bent on restoration.

Following breakfast, Jesus took Peter aside. What followed was an amazing conversation. Three times Jesus asked Peter if he loved Him. Three times Peter declared his love for Christ. Each declaration was echoed by a commissioning for Peter to care for Christ's followers.

I believe Jesus asked Peter to state his position three times for three reasons. First, it was Jesus' way of approaching the subject of Peter's betrayal. Peter was already repentant. The Scriptures say that as soon as the cock began to crow, Peter went out and wept bitterly. Christ didn't need to break Peter, but they did need to talk about the past and their future relationship. By asking Peter about his devotion to Christ three times, Christ revealed He knew of Peter's betrayal. As Peter himself said, "Lord, you know all things" (John 21:17b).

Second, I believe Peter needed the opportunity to reaffirm his devotion for Christ. In this conversation Jesus gave Peter that opportunity. Jesus knew Peter's heart was devoted to Him. Jesus didn't need to hear Peter reaffirm his love for Him, but He knew that Peter needed to hear himself put his feelings into words.

Third, Peter needed to know that Jesus didn't intend their relationship to end on a note of defeat. Jesus had a future for Peter. He wanted to use him. Every time Peter reaffirmed his love for Christ, Christ reaffirmed His commission to Peter.

What a beautiful challenge this friendship presents. Jesus was there that morning not to rebuke, but to rebuild. Ever so gently He guided Peter along a conversation that knit their hearts together again. Oh, that we would seek the counsel of the Prince of Peace when friendships rupture and confrontation becomes a necessity! Oh, that we would learn to set aside our own hurt for the sake of gaining back a brother or sister!

A Lesson in Vulnerability

The other challenge of these stories is simply that we are all vulnerable to temptation. Given the right conditions, none of us is immune. There is no room for haughtiness or self-sufficiency in the Christian walk.

It took me awhile to recover from the unfair tongue lashing I received that Sunday evening so long ago. Yet when the dust of my anger settled, I admit that if it had been possible to change places, I, too, might well have been tempted to judge a pastor's wife who was so different from what I'd expected. On the other hand, she may have been equally understanding of my need to find alternatives to a difficult situation. When we take the time to humble ourselves, when we take the time to care, we will finally realize we are all vulnerable to failure.

MAKING IT YOURS

1. Read John 8:1-11. If the evidence against this woman was true—and we've no reason to doubt it wasn't—were the Pharisees right in judging her? Explain.

2. Why didn't Jesus condemn her? (Also see John 1:17)

3. Did Jesus address the "sin" question? Explain.

4. Why did Jesus come into human history? (Luke 4:16-21; 19:10)

5. How is a critical attitude toward others evidence that we've been deceived by Satan?

6. How did Jesus deal with the rupture in their friendship that Peter's betrayal had caused?

7. What guidelines for confrontation does Paul offer in Galatians 6:1?

8. What principles did Jesus demonstrate in His confrontation with Peter that you can apply to relationships in your life?

Chapter Four

A Change of Heart

IT WAS ONLY A PLATE OF COOKIES and a Christmas card. But wrapped along with this neighborly gift was a story sad enough to dampen my best yuletide spirit.

Tony and Cassie had been our neighbors since moving to this small community. We'd become acquainted in a neighborly sort of way, and over time a rough friendship had sprung up between us. But when Tony arranged to have his wife arrested for failing to report to her parole officer, we were truly shocked. We came to understand Tony's true motivation when a gorgeous brunette moved in with Tony on the same day Cassie was arrested. It was certainly the biggest scandal to have rocked this sleepy town for some time. And the gossip it provided helped relieve the otherwise rainy monotony of the winter season.

But personally I felt only regret and confusion as

I accepted the card and cookies from Tony's girlfriend that night. A simple note was written inside the card: "We hope you have a very, merry Christmas and a wonderful New Year. Our whole family shall be joining your church soon."

"We've got to do something about this," I gasped to my husband. "We can't just let Tony and his girlfriend join the church as if that will whitewash everything!" He agreed, of course. After discussing the situation, we decided that my husband would talk with Tony. What's more, we began praying for our neighbors as we never had before.

Tony and my husband did talk. But soon other things began to happen, as well. Cassie was released on bail and moved back home. Tony's girlfriend temporarily made other arrangements.

Things were tense on the other side of the fence. Tony told my husband repeatedly that he was going to leave his wife. Several times we watched Tony load his pickup truck in preparation of the move he'd threatened. Yet, for some reason, Tony stayed.

Neither Cassie or Tony had ever seemed open to spiritual things. So I was taken back when Cassie called one night in tears and asked to talk with my husband. That evening Cassie gave her heart unreservedly to Jesus Christ. Her sentencing in court was only a few days away. She knew she would have six to eight months to serve. She knew how Tony would fill her place. And she doubted there would be a welcome home when her sentence was finished.

The details differ of course, but Tony and Cassie's saga of unfaithfulness and marital strife is played out repeatedly in homes across America. Not that we should find this shocking as Christians, for the Bible tells us that from the outset, man is doomed to failure. Estranged from God through our inherited sin nature, we are unable to fully realize all that God intends for our relationships. In fact, the Bible tells us we are motivated away from God by three sinful inborn motivations. First John 2:16 identifies our problem this way: "For all that is in the world, the lust of the flesh and the lust of the eyes and the boastful pride of life is not from the Father, but is from the world" (NASB).

There you have it—spiritual failure in a nutshell. And although these base motivations may propel one to personal worldly success, they invariably propel the majority to disaster, accompanied by painful personal consequences.

It is a bleak situation, except for the wonderful grace of Jesus Christ. For through Him we find victory over sin. And as our life comes under His touch, these inner motivations are changed. In Christ we are set free from the bonds of sin that lead to failure; set free to be all that God created and intends us to be.

God Replaces Lust with Love

Such was the experience of a woman who had spent her life in prostitution. The story is told in Luke 7:36-50.

Jesus had been invited to a Pharisee's home (Simon) for dinner. A select group of others were there as well. As the meal progressed, a prostitute managed to make her way into their presence.

Interestingly her response to Jesus was one of

deepest humility. She said and asked nothing of Him. Instead she knelt at His feet and began to weep. As she wept, she wet His feet with her tears and wiped them with her hair. Then, producing an alabaster vial, she anointed Christ's feet with expensive perfume.

This was a woman of the streets—a known prostitute! Why did she come to Jesus? We aren't told how she knew Him. Maybe she had heard Jesus speak or witnessed one of the miracles of healing He was so well known for. Or perhaps a friend had told her about this man that was so unlike any she had ever known. And so she came. Steeling herself against the gossip and ridicule she knew she would hear, she knelt humbly, publicly, and ministered to Jesus. She, who had spent her entire adult life lusting after men, now ministered from a heart overflowing with love. She was a new woman.

Jesus knew her reputation. He knew the record of sin against her seemed almost endless. But as she humbled herself before Him, Jesus did what no man had ever done before—Jesus gave her a new beginning.

He addressed her in three brief statements:
"Your sins are forgiven" (7:48).
"Your faith has saved you" (7:50).
"Go in peace" (7:50).
What a remarkable gift these words contain! Forgiveness—the past and all its humiliation was gone forever. She had been saved from her hopeless enslavement to lust. Instead, her actions became a permanent example of pure love; a story included in the Gospel record for all time. And she was given

peace—inner peace from all the pressures and condemnation her life had known.

God Replaces Greed with a Giving Spirit

Jesus transformed another unlikely person's life. This time it was a despised tax collector, Zacchaeus.

Zacchaeus had a job nobody liked. He collected taxes from his fellow Jewish citizens in Jericho for the Roman government. Because of this role, he was seen as a traitor to the Jewish community. And he probably would have found it difficult to hold his job against such hostile public opinion, but his greed outweighed his pride. Tax collectors were allowed to charge more tax than was due. The surplus became the income of the collector. Zacchaeus saw to it that his job was well worth the social rejection. As a result, he became a wealthy, if somewhat lonely, man.

One day news reached Zacchaeus that Jesus was coming to Jericho. A great crowd turned out to welcome Him. Zacchaeus went, too. Yet being short in stature, Zacchaeus was unable to see past the press of the crowd. Suddenly he noticed a sycamore tree overshadowing the walk up which Jesus was coming. Zacchaeus climbed to a perch above the crowd and watched.

Slowly Jesus made His way up the crowded street. When He got to the sycamore tree, He stopped and looked up at Zacchaeus and said, "Zacchaeus, come down immediately. I must stay at your house today" (Luke 19:5).

Can you imagine the shock that spread through that crowd? Jesus wanted to stay at Zacchaeus' house! It must have seemed an outrage! And when the shock wore off, no doubt some felt a bit miffed that Zacchaeus had been chosen to entertain Jesus when others seemed so much more deserving. It just didn't seem right.

Yet it was Zacchaeus Jesus was interested in. And Zacchaeus welcomed Christ's suggestion. Zacchaeus quickly scrambled from his perch, and they were soon on their way to his home.

I often wonder how I would have responded if I had been in Zacchaeus' shoes that day? I imagine my response would have been something like this: "You want to come to my house, Jesus? And You want to come now—today? Well, that would be great but . . . Maybe we could have lunch together next week sometime. You see, uh, I've got a lot going on right now. It would be so much better if You could let me know a little ahead of time when You want to visit. As it is, I just don't think today will work out."

Perhaps your response would be similar. Why? Because we know that to fellowship with Christ is to place ourselves under His influence—an influence that may bring conviction to our hearts.

Such was the case with Zacchaeus. As he and Jesus walked toward his home, Zacchaeus recognized and repented of his life of greed. "Look, Lord!" Zacchaeus said, "Here and now I give half of my possessions to the poor, and if I have cheated anybody out of anything, I will pay back four times the amount" (19:8). Zacchaeus was a changed man! Instead of being the biggest crook in Jericho, he became the town's leading philanthropist! Amazing? Yes. Unbelievable? Not when Christ is welcomed into a person's life. Under His touch, inner motivations of a lifetime are changed in an instant. But I also observe here a lesson in the attitude of the crowd. They did not approve of Zacchaeus' change of heart. The Bible says that when the townspeople saw Jesus leave with Zacchaeus they "began to mutter, 'He has gone to be the guest of a "sinner" ' " (19:7). Why did they disapprove? As we mentioned earlier, it may have been surprise or wounded egos. For some Zacchaeus' conversion may also have been a threat. Up to this point Zacchaeus had filled a niche of hatred in Jericho's social circles. Should he change, the entire town would have to change their attitudes about Zacchaeus as well. He would no longer be a safe target of gossip. He might need to be included in social settings from which he was previously exiled. What's worse, he might change in a way that would challenge their own faith and morality.

The change Christ makes is not only a personal phenomenon, but a social one as well. This fact hit home for me one Sunday morning, soon after two young women in our town had come to know Christ. They had been transformed. Joy and peace radiated from their lives and lips. True to their conversion, they had also become regular church attenders. It was exciting to see the change Christ was making in their lives. And we as a church were excited with them—most of us, that is. There was, unfortunately, one couple who didn't approve.

The wife caught up with me after church one Sunday morning. "I can't believe she's here!" she said with unmistakable disapproval.

"Oh, you mean Trish?" I said. "Well, you probably

haven't heard. Trish received Christ several weeks ago. She and her friend have been attending very regularly since then."

"Well," the indignant woman said, "I never dreamed I'd see her here! I've had occasion to deal with her before, and she was almost rude!"

"Yes, well, she's changed since she came to Christ," I countered. "She's a completely new person—they both are. Personally, I think it's really exciting!"

"Yeah. I guess so," she responded sourly.

Interestingly that couple never returned to our church again. I can only speculate that, in part, a change in attitude proved too great an obstacle.

Most "cold shouldering" isn't so obvious. Rather it is the dinner invitations that never come. It is the lacking word of welcome, or allowing our new Christian brother or sister to sit alone while we sit with those we are more comfortable with. Sometimes it is a disapproving word concerning their zeal for the Lord. May God forgive us if we've played the part of the Jericho townspeople, unwilling to adjust our social attitudes to accept one the Lord Himself accepts. May God grant us the humbleness of heart to welcome the challenges changed lives present.

God Blesses the Humble not the Proud

The last story I want to look at was actually a parable told by Jesus. It is recorded for us in Luke 18:9–14. The story goes that two men went to the temple to pray. One man was a tax collector, a known sinner and despised by his community. The other man was a respected Pharisee.

The prayer of the Pharisee is recorded first. It went like this:

> God, I thank you that I am not like other men—robbers, evildoers, adulterers—or even like this tax collector. I fast twice a week and give a tenth of all I get. (18:11-12)

Jesus told the prayer of the tax collector next. It was a simple prayer: "God, have mercy on me, a sinner" (18:13).

Only one man went home changed that day, Jesus told the crowd. That man was the tax collector. "For," Jesus concluded, "everyone who exalts himself will be humbled, and he who humbles himself will be exalted" (18:14).

When we come face to face with God's holiness and our neediness, there is no room for arrogance. This was the lesson King Nebuchadnezzar learned when God humbled him through a seven year lapse into insanity (Daniel 4:34-37). It was the realization that wrought tortured and penitent words from the prophet Isaiah (Isaiah 6:1-7). In fact, wherever God's presence was revealed throughout Scripture, a holy, terrifying awe and reverence followed.

That God invites us to enjoy a personal relationship with Him is indeed an incredible privilege. Never will we receive an invitation of greater honor. That God also doesn't insist on a humble response of gratitude is an equal wonder. He will allow us to go arrogantly on our way. For awhile at least, He will wait for a change of heart. But when we truly turn and seek Him, God meets us and, in His presence, arrogance evaporates into deepest humility. The depth of our humility is dependent only upon one factor, the sincerity of our search to know God. For the more we know Him, the greater our awe, the more distant any thought of arrogant self-rule.

The path to humility is not without cost, however. It cost the tax collector a lot to share the temple with the Pharisee that day. He was ridiculed. He became emotional; something many of us fear in a social setting. But the cost didn't matter to the tax collector. Unlike the Pharisee, he was in the temple because he wanted to get right with God. What others thought was irrelevant.

I wonder who we are praying to when we're at church? Are we there to truly worship; even at the expense of our egos, if need be? It seems altar calls in church services are quickly becoming a thing of the past. Admittedly they can be overdone. Emotional manipulation is never the same as true conversion. Yet I wonder if, as churches, we do our congregations a disservice by withholding occasional opportunities for people to publicly humble themselves before God and seek His face. Are such calls difficult to respond to? Intensely so, but God honors the one who will seek Him at all costs. First Peter 5:5-6 advises: "God opposes the proud/ but gives grace to the humble. Humble yourselves, therefore, under God's mighty hand, that he may lift you up in due time."

In Jesus' parable, the tax collector alone went home a changed man. Quite simply, he was the only one who truly sought God.

The Miracle of Change

Jesus Christ changes lives because He changes the

very heart of man. The Bible says: "Therefore, if anyone is in Christ, he is a new creation; the old has gone, the new has come!" (2 Corinthians 5:17).

It is not a matter of restraining or remaking the old you. Christ does an entirely new creation in the heart that yields to Him.

Such was the case with Cassie. Soon after Cassie was incarcerated, God began impressing me that I should go and visit her. "But, God," I argued, "do I have to? I've never visited anyone in jail before! I won't know how to act—what to say." It all seemed demeaning somehow. Yet I couldn't ignore the urgings of God's Spirit. When I finally went and discovered I could get clearance as a chaplain to go into the prisoners' living areas, I was ever more reticent.

I certainly never bargained for this as a pastor's wife, I thought to myself as I showed my pass to the guard watching me by monitor. A buzz and red light indicated that another door in the maze to the inner jail was being unlocked. As I stepped through, I prayed, "O God, I'm so grateful that I can leave this place when my visit is over. I certainly hope You don't intend this to be an ongoing area of ministry for me!"

Cassie met me eagerly behind the final set of steel doors. She introduced me to the other women in the jail. As I looked at the circle of curious faces, I kept wondering just what specifically had brought these women here. I also kept hoping my good neighbor was not handing out my address and phone number. It was certainly a tense visit.

But in the weeks and months that followed, the routine became familiar, and God's hand undeniable. Rather than dreading my jail visits, I began to anticipate them eagerly. For Cassie was growing in her faith. She was attending a Bible study that the chaplain provided and doing additional reading on her own. She was studying to get her G.E.D. and took advantage of the opportunity to receive counseling in areas of need. And Cassie began to pray. She told me, "I don't know if Tony will ever take me back. I'm praying he will. But if he doesn't, I know I've got God. He's all I need."

At home, Tony's affair had dissolved as his girlfriend went on to become attracted to someone else. He was ashamed, bitter and angry. After a few weeks, he tried visiting Cassie. But with the glass barricade between them, it seemed too difficult and humiliating. He told her he'd never be back.

Yet back Tony came. Not just for visits, but sending her romantic cards as well. Then came a day when Cassie pulled me aside. "I've got something to tell you," she confided eagerly. "Tony came to visit last night. He asked me to forgive him. Then he asked me to marry him all over again. When I get out, he's going to talk to your husband about renewing our wedding vows." Tears of joy filled my eyes. God had done a miracle in Cassie's marriage! This was a day of joy for both of us.

"What do you think has made the change in Tony?" I asked Cassie.

A smile spread across her face. "Prayer made the difference. Your husband was right. I just needed to turn it all over to Christ!"

Tony and Cassie moved away shortly after she was released. They said they wanted a fresh start far away from gossiping tongues. Before they left, they both thanked us for our friendship. And on a visit to the area a year later, Cassie stopped by to tell me what God was continuing to do in her life. She was still Cassie; a little rough and tough around the edges, as she probably always will be. But there was a warm inner glow to her life as well—the undeniable fragrance of Jesus Christ. Without a doubt, Cassie had become a new woman.

And there have been countless others whose lives have been equally transformed by Jesus Christ—others like Karen. Before Karen gave her life to Christ she was a tough and bitter woman. Life was hard for her. She and her husband had two boys—one, theirs, and one, hers by a previous marriage. And although they had custody, visitation rights with her ex-husband had caused endless conflict. Finances were also a problem, and the demands of Karen's full-time job just added to the stress level at home.

Now it just so happened that a close friend of Karen's had received Christ the previous summer. As Karen watched, her friend's life began to change. Karen became curious. Slowly she began to long for spiritual reality in her own life as well.

Then one day my phone rang. It was Karen's friend. "Karen wants to hear how to receive Christ. I'd tell her myself, but I don't know all the right words. I'm afraid I'd mess it all up. Would you come over and talk with her?" I agreed.

Later as I sat on the sofa next to Karen and shared the gospel, I could tell the Holy Spirit was working in her heart. When I finished sharing and invited her to pray committing her life to Christ, the words came easily and the tears flowed freely. Karen was a new woman.

Karen's new identity in Christ became increasingly obvious in the days and months that followed. Co-workers began to question her about the difference in her life. "What's with you?" they would ask. "Why are you smiling all the time?" Then Karen would share with them the miracle of her new life in Jesus Christ.

Other things changed, too. She found patience to wait on God to make her husband receptive to spiritual things. She found the courage to make a stand for honesty at work, and forgo work relationships that revolved around gossip. Karen began attending church regularly, taking her boys with her. She took part in a women's Bible study and became a prayer partner for one of the church's evangelistic visitation teams. She was simply not the same person. God had worked a miracle.

How does this all relate to the topic of success and failure? Quite simply there is no true success apart from Jesus Christ. We all need a change of heart spiritually, and He is the only Surgeon that can do the job.

What if we've already given our heart to Christ, but allowed other things to cool our love for Him? If this is so, we need to humble ourselves before God, renewing our focus on our new identity in Christ. New birth, after all, is just a start. Learning to walk in our new identity is the next step on the path to successfully becoming all God intends us to be.

MAKING IT YOURS

1. Define "spiritual failure" in a nutshell. (1 John 2:16)

2. Read Luke 7:36-50. What was the woman's past reputation?

3. How was she changed by her humble worship of Jesus? (Luke 7:47-50)

4. Now read Luke 19:1-10. What was Zacchaeus' local reputation?

5. How did his lifestyle change as Zacchaeus met Jesus?

6. How did the townspeople react to Zacchaeus' decision to receive Christ?

7. How is conversion a social change as well as a personal one? (Ephesians 2:17-20)

8. Read Luke 18:9-14. Briefly describe the Pharisee and the tax collector.

9. Which man left the temple a changed man? Why?

10. What hope for success does 1 Corinthians 5:17 hold out to everyone who yields his or her life to Christ?

Chapter Five

Switching Places

IN MARK TWAIN'S WELL-KNOWN STORY, "The Prince and the Pauper," an incredible exchange of identities takes place. The prince, tired of the academic routine of the palace, meets and switches places with a look-alike beggar boy. The results are dramatic. Both boys are exposed, for the first time, to a side of life never experienced before—the prince to the hardships of the street and common life, the beggar boy to the richness of life as royalty (Twain 1954).

Although it's just a story, Twain's tale does in some ways mirror an exchange of identities that continues to happen even today. It is summarized for us in Second Corinthians 5:21: "God made [Christ] who had no sin to be sin for us, so that in [Christ] we might become the righteousness of God." When Christ became man and took our sinful place at Calvary, He offered us a wonderful exchange of identity. In a very real sense the King of kings became sin that we might be transformed into royalty ourselves. This is what Paul meant when he wrote: "If anyone is in Christ, he is a new creation; the old has gone, the new has come" (2 Corinthians 5:17). It's an incredible fact—the old you is gone forever! By placing our faith in Christ's death for our sin, our spiritual identity changes from that of the condemned to that of a forgiven and true member of God's household.

Why is it then that many Christians seem little different from non-Christians? And if we define success as faithfully living in obedience to God, is such a lifestyle consistently possible? These are good questions. If you are like most Christians, you may have wrestled with these, and related questions repeatedly. That a faithful Christian life experience is possible seems logical. Otherwise God would never have provided the Holy Spirit to enable us to walk with Him. But let's start by addressing the first question. Why is it that Christians and non-Christians often seem so much alike?

Is There a Visible Difference?

When I was a kid, my parents owned a trailer at a lake resort. Every summer our family would move from our home in the city to the lake. There my two brothers and I joined the other kids in the resort in all sorts of adventures. Of course while we were on the lake, fishing always filled a good portion of our time. And as the summers passed, we became experts at catching grasshoppers for bait.

Now grasshoppers are amazing bugs. You can catch one fairly easily. And as long as you keep your fingers curled tightly over it (and don't mind a little bug spit), your grasshopper won't get away. I've even seen some that go into a state of shock sit in an open palm for a short while. But once a grasshopper has an "out" and recognizes it, he springs away in a mighty leap.

The grasshopper reminds me of my life in Christ. When I received Christ, I voluntarily placed myself in God's hands. Unlike a fisherman's grasshopper, I was safe and loved in my Father's care. Yet too often I began to look at the circumstances around me. Things often looked threatening. Slowly I allowed mistrust to creep into my thoughts. Secretly I began to wonder, *Is God really to be trusted with this situation? Does He really know what's best for me?* Often in a moment of panic, so much like the bewildered grasshopper, I would spring away from God. Forsaking my refuge in Him, I jumped into my life of challenges to meet them the best I could. In so doing, I forsook the identity Christ had given me.

For example, when I say that God opened another door of opportunity, you must understand that the "opportunity" God placed before us appeared far from golden to me. We had been seeking an associate position in a larger church in the Pacific Northwest. What God provided, couldn't have seemed more different.

"What would you think about moving to Omaha, Nebraska, for a year?" my husband asked me as I ferried loaded suitcases to the car. I was taking the children on a brief vacation to eastern Washington to visit their grandparents. "Tom Stebbins, the outreach pastor at Christ Community Church, thinks it would be an invaluable experience for me to intern under him for a year.'"

"Omaha!" I responded unenthusiastically. "I don't even know where that is!" Nor were my additional comments any more positive. Finally, I promised my husband I'd think about it while I was away.

And think about it I did. All the way to eastern Washington I mentally debated this intern "opportunity." It certainly fell far short of what I'd expected as our next move. Scott's internship would mean he'd have to work a second job to support us. There was little salary available to interns. It would mean driving all our belongings (plus two kids and a cat) across the country and finding a place to live within two to three days before we had to return the rented truck. Emotionally, I expected such a year to be terribly lonely. There just wouldn't be enough time and security for developing close friendships. And at the end of the year, we'd have to renew our job search, and move all over again.

The more I thought about this opportunity, the angrier I became. I was angry at God for not opening the way to something more in line with my expectations. And I was angry at my husband that he would even consider this a golden opportunity! I began to wonder seriously if I hadn't made a big mistake when I married Scott. After all, his career and my expectations hardly seemed headed in the same direction.

Although I was angry and frightened by the unknowns of our future, God reasoned with my heart that week. Over the months ahead, God began to build in my heart a tremendous sense of anticipation for the adventure ahead. And as for any thoughts of divorce—a week's vacation as a single parent to two preschoolers was enough to convince me that divorce was too high a price to pay to stay anywhere in particular!

Like the fisherman's grasshopper, in fear I had temporarily sprung away from a place of rest in the Father's hands. But if I had continued in my independent thinking, my royal heritage in Christ would have begun to fade. In time my life would never have reflected the true child of God that I really am. And this is how many Christians come to appear like non-Christians. Quite simply, they've forsaken their identity in Jesus Christ.

To live as God intends, we must continue to grow into our new identity. All the aspects of our identity are current factual realities. We are completely new in Christ (2 Corinthians 5:17). We have moved from a position of divine rejection to one of complete acceptance (Romans 8:1). We have all we need to be complete in Christ (Colossians 2:10). We have bold and confident access to God as our Heavenly Father (Ephesians 3:12). And we have the certainty of a life of spiritual productivity (John 15:5). But knowing these (and the other facts of our new identity) is not enough. We must daily and willfully claim these realities by faith. How does this happen?

Desire

A consistent walk with Christ happens only as we apply three key steps. The first of these is coming to a place where we *desire* to walk with Christ, to seek to experientially share His identity. Jesus said, "Blessed are those who hunger and thirst for righteousness, for they will be filled" (Matthew 5:6).

There is nothing so compelling as true hunger or thirst. Such a craving demands satisfaction. These cravings are inborn survival instincts that protect the essence of life itself. Jesus was drawing a spiritual parallel. He was simply saying, blessed are those who have come to a place of undeniable spiritual craving, for they will discover satisfaction in God.

How does a person develop such a craving? The answer quite simply is to heighten your awareness of need. This in part is the ministry of the Holy Spirit. Just as you don't work at producing a feeling of physical hunger or thirst (unless you are dieting, of course), neither do you produce a sense of spiritual thirst. Rather, this desire for God is a craving that grows through our walk with God. Jesus said:

> When [the Holy Spirit] comes, he will convict the world of guilt in regard to sin and righteousness and judgment: . . . in regard to righteousness, because I am going to the Father, where you can see me no longer. (John 16:8-10)

The Holy Spirit is given to each believer to convict of guilt in regard to righteous living. The experiences of guilt and conviction in turn produce a recognition of our need for God. Once the need is acknowledged, spiritual hunger and thirst follow.

Like the prodigal son, we have each wandered away from home. In love and wisdom, the Father lets us go. He knows this is the only way we will truly begin to hunger and thirst for Him. When we hit bottom on the dregs of our selfish waywardness and the Holy Spirit brings us to our senses, we'll long to return humbly home to stay. This was the message echoed by the prophet Jeremiah when he rebuked Judah for their lapse into idolatry. Jeremiah warned:

> Your own wickedness will correct you,
> And your apostasies will reprove you;
> Know therefore and see that it is evil and bitter
> For you to forsake the LORD your God.
> (Jeremiah 2:19, NASB)

Interestingly, spiritual failure and spiritual success seem interdependent. We cannot hunger for God unless we become aware of our own sinfulness. Ironically it is through our failing that God trains us to walk with Him.

There are, of course, two kinds of God-directed discipline. Some discipline is earned as a result of intentional rebellion on our part. This was the kind of discipline the Lord proclaimed through Jeremiah.

The other discipline is conviction that comes as a result of our growing understanding of God. For the Holy Spirit came to be our instructor as well as our conscience. John 16:13 says that "the Spirit of truth . . . will guide you into all truth." As we read God's word, the Holy Spirit shows us areas in our life that need to change. God's Word is like a mirror. As we read, and consider our life before God, it is as if we are looking at our reflection. We see the changes God has made. Also reflected, however, are the imperfections still to be dealt with. This process of exposing ourselves to God and the conviction such exposure brings will make us recognize our need and hunger for Him.

Another way we come to hunger and thirst for God is to simply ask for it. David admitted such a need in his penitent Psalm. In it he prayed: "Restore to me the joy of your salvation and grant me a willing spirit, to sustain me" (51:12).

These are interesting words from a man who described his thirst for God as a deer panting for water. (42:1) But you see, David recognized he needed a willing spirit to seek after spiritual things. David realized that such a will was not naturally his own. He knew that only a God-given thirst would sustain his walk with God.

Humble Confession

The next step in walking with God is simply an outgrowth of conviction. That step is confession. Once we become aware of our need for God, it is time to right the broken relationship we have with Him. Like the father of the prodigal son, God waits longingly to gather us in His arms of compassion; to forgive us and welcome us home. How sad that our pride often keeps us so far away in spiritual poverty.

The difficulty of confession struck me in a deeper way one afternoon. My daughter and I were talking in the kitchen. For some reason her mood was sullen and Sierra began to talk to me in a disrespectful manner. Now a disrespectful attitude is something that is not tolerated in our home. As I called this attitude to Sierra's attention, I told her she was wrong to talk to me that way and that I expected an apology. I told her she was to think about what she had said and then say: "I'm sorry. Would you please forgive me?"

What ensued was remarkable. The words, "I'm sorry," came out rather quickly. But Sierra was hesitant to ask my forgiveness. We talked about the situation. She knew she had been wrong and was clearly miserable by the breach in our relationship, but her pride still stood in the way. This intense impasse between the two of us went on for nearly 45 minutes.

Finally I said, "Why don't you just come out and say, 'Please forgive me'? I will forgive you. I want to forgive you and give you a big hug. Why don't you just say it and get it over with?"

Sierra tearfully responded: "I will say, 'I'm sorry. Please forgive me.' But I don't want any hugs!"

Humility is so hard, isn't it? And yet our loving Heavenly Father longs to gather us in His arms, to forgive us and hold us close, even as I did with my own daughter that afternoon.

What's more, the Bible promises:

> For Thou, Lord, art good, and ready to forgive,
> And abundant in loving kindness to all who call
> upon Thee. (86:5, NASB)

> The sacrifices of God are a broken spirit;
> a broken and contrite heart,
> O God, you will not despise. (51:17)

The second key to walking in our new identity in Christ, then, is humble confession. God waits to welcome us. We only need to come.

A Commitment to Obedience

Lastly, walking with God involves a commitment to obedience. I remember driving through a remote logging town in the mountains of northern Idaho. One main road led through the community. Two taverns (one on either side of town) served as combination gas stations, restaurants, bars and social centers. They were, in fact, the only businesses in town! Needing gas, I stopped at one tavern and filled up. But as I entered to pay, I saw a sign I've never forgotten. Nailed there next to the door were these words: "Please Leave All Guns and Knives Outside." I've never paid for gas any quicker than I did that day!

I tell this story to underline the importance of commitment. If we are to walk in Christ's presence, there are things that must be left outside our lives. Colossians 3:8-10 says:

> But now you must rid yourselves of all such things as these: anger, rage, malice, slander, and filthy language from your lips. Do not lie to each other, since you have taken off your old self with its practices and have put on the new self, which is being renewed in knowledge in the image of its Creator.

How do we leave these things outside our lives? We do so by willfully deciding to identify with Christ instead of our old way of life. Galatians 5:16 says, "live by the Spirit, and you will not gratify the desires of the sinful nature." This is the core truth of abiding in Christ. Jesus illustrated this lesson using the example of a grapevine in John 15. When a branch remains grafted to the vine, the life of the vine flows through the branch producing fruit. The identities of the two parts are one and the same. Should the same branch be cut from the vine, it would wither and die, fruitless and worthless.

God will allow countless crises to come into our lives to teach us to remain grafted to Him. I believe this was one reason our first pastorate in western Washington was so difficult for me. I wanted to be the perfect pastor's wife on my own strength. God knew I needed to learn to depend and draw solely on Him. A rhetorical question shared with me by a counselor I was seeing at that time has helped me time and again to personalize this concept of abiding in Christ. When I would share with her a seemingly insurmountable situation I was facing, she would simply remind me, "Cheryl, where do you get your life?" The answer should be obvious. Colossians 3:3 says, "For you [have] died and your life is now hidden with Christ in God."

We get our life from Jesus Christ. When life's circumstances or temptations seem insurmountable, we need to consciously remind ourselves that life is not to be found in those things. Jesus is our life. No matter what happens, He will take care of us. We dare not jump out of Christ's presence like a mindless grasshopper escaping on instinct. Our old instincts are warped by sin. If we follow them we will certainly end up far from God and all He longs for us to experience. Instead, we must learn to respond anew, to respond according to faith.

The move to Omaha, Nebraska, was an immense

step of faith for me. Before we left I often had nightmares we'd get stuck in a blizzard out there on the road somewhere. (And we did get snowed in overnight in Gillette, Wyoming!) And when we arrived and were temporarily settled again, I remember wondering if this adventure was really going to pay off. "God," I prayed, "make this a significant year for my husband; worth every sacrifice. But, Lord, make it a significant year for the rest of us as well."

And God did just that. In that year God opened the way for me to write a column for a ministry wives' magazine, author this book, teach a women's Bible study at Christ Community Church and travel with my husband to help share the gospel in St. Croix. My husband received an invaluable year of training in outreach ministry and the thrill of establishing a new church in Missouri Valley, Iowa. We developed new friendships. Our neighbors came to Christ, as well as countless others. And the blessings that God poured out on our children are beyond numbering. What's more, at year's end, God led us right back to our beloved Pacific Northwest.

Oh, what we would have missed if I'd dug in my heels and refused to move! I'm so glad I took the moment to ask for faith before I jumped away from God's care.

Stumbling and then thirsting; humbling ourselves and confessing our need for Him; deciding to be obedient and abiding by faith in Christ's presence— these are the steps on the path to experientially exchanging your old identity for the new one Christ has given you.

Where do you stand? What are you pursuing as the source of life? Are you submitting your identity to Christ? Are you seeking to exchange your poverty for the limitless riches of Jesus Christ?

Exchanging your identity for that of Jesus Christ also entitles you to share His power. No one is more aware of this than Satan. After all, watching you produce spiritual fruit is the last thing he wants to happen. If Satan can't tempt you away from walking with Christ, he'll certainly do his best to see you get hung up along the way. One way Satan does that is by deceiving you into taking a "guilt trip." Some of us have been on such "trips" for years. And they are no vacation, believe me! What we need to know is how to cancel our "guilt trip" reservations. And this is just the subject we'll look at next.

MAKING IT YOURS

1. How did Christ exchange indentities with us? (2 Corinthians 5:21)

2. If Christians have exchanged identities with Christ, why is it that many believers seem little different from non-believers?

3. What is the first step in growing into our new identity in Christ?

4. How does God use our failures to produce a desire to walk with Him? (Jeremiah 2:19)

5. What is the second step in growing into our new identity in Christ?

6. What is God's promised response to the humble and repentant heart? (Psalm 51:17; Psalm 86:5; 1 John 1:9)

7. What decision will enable us to consistently live out our new identity in Christ?

8. What do you think it means to die and hide your life in Christ? (Colossians 3:3)

Chapter Six

How to Cancel a Guilt Trip

STATISTICS SHOW THAT THE WESTERN states have the highest incidence of suicide in the nation. (Although Washington and Oregon don't have the highest suicide rate, as many suppose. Alaska holds that questionable honor. [*Statistical Abstract of the United States* 1990, 82]) Still, the West's higher rate of suicide certainly proved itself true in our community.

In the four years that we pastored in a small town in western Washington (approximately 1,000 population), we had contact with 10 completed or attempted suicides! Almost half of these, at one time or another, lived in our immediate neighborhood. The suicide I remember most vividly, however, didn't happen during the dreary, wet, winter season. Instead, it scored itself across my memory one cloudless, hot, summer afternoon.

My husband, Scott, had suggested we go see the

waterfall and fish ladder near town. In early autumn the migrating salmon congregate at the base of the falls. From there they try to migrate up the falls in a series of vain, but spectacular, leaps. It is always an amazing sight.

This day, however, we were disappointed when we reached the base of the falls. Today, there were no salmon in sight. The scenery was beautiful, however, and we lingered a few moments to just enjoy the day.

All at once our thoughts were shattered by a blood-curdling scream. The falls descend in a series of cascading steps. The river drops over a series of large boulders, turns slightly and falls again. Above us on the rocky ledge overlooking the upper falls was a shrieking, screaming woman. Somehow she had managed to get behind a chain link fence that barricaded the area. She was obviously very distraught. Scott and I both feared that she was about to leap to her death in the icy water and rocks below.

"Hurry!" I urged my husband. "I think she's going to jump!"

Scott pushed our infant son into my arms and started across the rocks below the ledge where the shrieking woman stood. I took our children and started up the pathway and toward the car. If she did jump, I didn't want the children to see it.

Partway up I paused and looked down toward another area of the rocks below—a cleft among the boulders below the upper falls. A man's body lay motionless in the inlet. Scott scrambled across the spot about the same moment. By this time the local police chief had also arrived. He was soon beside Scott. Together they reached into the water and pulled out what was later discovered to be the fiancé of the screaming woman above.

Scott stayed and counseled with the woman. The story that unfolded was a sad tale. This couple and a friend had been using drugs in the woods nearby. After awhile they decided to hike to the waterfall. For some reason the boyfriend went ahead of the other two. When they reached the falls later, they couldn't find him. According to his fiancée, he had been talking about suicide often in recent weeks. After searching for awhile, they finally phoned the police. It was soon after that, that the current pushed his body in this backwater among the boulders. Whether he had intentionally jumped or simply slipped and fallen into the icy water was never known. What was known was that the desire to end life had been a regular part of his thoughts up to this point. He had even asked his fiancée to bury him in a trash dumpster when he died. Clearly he saw his life as worthless as garbage.

What propels a person to such hopelessness? There are many causes, of course. Yet guilt is among the leading symptoms of depression and causes of suicide. Guilt can wrap its icy grip around our psyche and nearly immobilize us. Erwin Lutzer, in his book *Failure: The Back Door to Success*, wrote:

> I am convinced that the greatest single cause of spiritual defeat is a guilty conscience. . . . Satan's strategy: he gets Christians to become preoccupied with their failures; from then on, the battle is won. (Lutzer 1975, 50, 51)

What great, good news it is to realize that Jesus came to set us free from the bondage of guilt! The Apostle Paul exults:

> Therefore, there is now no condemnation for those who are in Christ Jesus, because through Christ Jesus the law of the Spirit of life set me free from the law of sin and death. (Romans 8:1-2)

Satan may desire to "steal and kill and destroy"; but Jesus came to provide life in all its fullness (John 10:10).

Yet to fully experience this abundant life we must also deeply experience God's forgiveness. For it is only as we grasp the full picture of God's mercy that we can forgive others and forgive ourselves.

The Positive Side of Guilt

Like a coin, guilt has two sides—a positive, healthy side and a negative, crippling side. The healthy side we call *conscience*. Without a sense of conscience, we would all end up sociopaths and society, as we know it, wouldn't endure long. Indeed, we fear such individuals. Their crippled lives fill our prisons. A positive sense of guilt helps protect us and others from the consequences of unrestrained selfishness.

Guilt can be healthy when it leads us to *confession* and forgiveness. The Bible says: "If we confess our sins, he is faithful and just and will forgive us our sins and purify us from all unrighteousness" (1 John 1:9). If we will only come in repentance, God promises to justly and faithfully forgive.

It must have been a terrible shock to the disciples

during Passover in Jerusalem so long ago. Within a few days they lost two close friends. Jesus had died at the hands of wicked men to offer forgiveness. And Judas had died by his own hand because he could not forgive himself. Matthew records that when Judas realized Jesus' arrest was to end in His death "he was seized with remorse" (27:3). He tried to return the money given him by the chief priests and make things right but it was too late. Matthew 27:5 says: "So Judas threw the money into the temple and left. Then he went away and hanged himself."

What a tragedy! What Judas failed to realize, or failed to accept, was that all the time Christ's forgiveness was only a request away.

The day Christ was crucified, two thieves were crucified as well. Pushing himself up on his skewered feet, one man mocked: "Aren't you the Christ? Save yourself and us!" (Luke 23:39). But the other man's response was entirely different. "Don't you fear God," he said, "since you are under the same sentence? We are punished justly, for we are getting what our deeds deserve. But this man has done nothing wrong." Then he said, "Jesus, remember me when you come into your kingdom" (23:40-42).

This man was a criminal, justly condemned even by his own testimony. Yet Jesus' forgiveness was immediate and complete. "Jesus answered him, 'I tell you the truth, today you will be with me in paradise'" (23:43). Did you catch the significance of this promise? A clear conscience—peace with God—it is only a request away. If we ask for forgiveness, forgiveness is ours.

From Rejection to Acceptance

But before we move on too quickly, let's linger a moment longer at Calvary. For not only did Christ pay the price of sin that day, but in offering Himself in our place He also bore the full anger of God against sin.

Do you remember what it feels like to be rejected? Perhaps you recall a time in grade school when you weren't included in a schoolyard game or a secret shared among friends. Perhaps the word rejection recalls the bitterness of having a boyfriend break up with you for someone else. Or maybe you don't have to travel so far back in your memory banks to recall the inner anguish of rejection. It hurts so badly to be turned away, doesn't it?

I remember watching a professional football game on television one afternoon with my husband. The Chicago Bears were playing. I can't recall the other team, but the game was going badly for the Bears. Near the end of the game an inexperienced quarterback went in. Brashly he began ignoring the coach and calling the plays himself. I suppose if the Bears had gained some yardage, the quarterback's brashness wouldn't have been so bad; but such was not the case. When a time out was finally called and the quarterback jogged to the sideline, the coach was furious!

What followed was a gesture more eloquent, more powerful, than any string of curses. Rather than bawl him out, the coach turned away, refusing to face his quarterback for the entire time out! I'm sure many were laughing; but not the quarterback. He stood there helplessly. The coach's message was clear—"I don't even want to talk to you!" Now that's rejection!

Christ, on the other hand, had always experienced total acceptance by God the Father. Imagine, if you can, a relationship so perfect that for all eternity there is never a difference of opinion, never an argument. In fact, although we can't understand it, the Bible tells us that Christ and God are one. They have the perfect harmonious relationship.

But when Christ allowed Himself to be forced upon the cross, He voluntarily placed Himself in the path of His Father's total rejection. The One who had never experienced a fractured relationship now knew in full force the pain of total separation. From His lips came the tortured cry, "My God, my God, why have you forsaken me?" (Matthew 27:46b). God the Father had turned away from Jesus the Son.

Our relationship with God radically changed in that moment. The Bible says that when Jesus died, the curtain separating the Holy of holies in the temple from the outer court was torn in two (27:51). Prior to this only the high priest was admitted once a year to make sacrifices on behalf of the people. Now admittance to the presence of God was open to all. No longer did man need to cower before God the Father, vainly offering sacrifices for his sin. The era of sacrifice ended in the perfect sacrifice of Jesus Christ. At the cross God's wrath was fully satisfied. God's forgiveness replaced our guilt. His acceptance displaced rejection. Today, because of Christ, we can enter instantly and confidently into the presence of Almighty God (Hebrews 10:19-22).

The Negative Side of Guilt

Satan's skill at deception is the third reason people struggle with guilt feelings. And make no mistake, Satan is good at making things appear as they aren't! Paul warned the Christians at Corinth that Satan can disguise himself even "as an angel of light" (2 Corinthians 11:14). And Jesus called Satan "the father of lies" (John 8:44). So it is no surprise that he comes whispering deceptions into the minds of God's children—lies even about feelings of guilt.

Perhaps you have heard his voice. He comes to you at a point of weakness or defeat with thoughts similar to these:

"I can't believe you've done that again! You'll never have victory. Why don't you just give up?"

"I thought you called yourself a Christian? Real Christians don't do those things. You must not be saved after all."

"You can't expect God to forgive you forever! Why don't you come back when you are serious about dealing with this, huh?"

"Well, God may forgive, but what about restitution? I mean, don't you think you ought to try and make it up to Him somehow?"

Satan is a liar and a deceiver. What's more, Christians are his favorite targets. Revelation 12:10 identifies Satan as "the accuser of our brothers." He doesn't accuse non-Christians. They pose no threat to Satan's realm. But the Christian is another matter. It wouldn't be good for Satan at all if believers realized their deliverance from sin and began sharing that message with others. So he concentrates all his deceptive powers to discourage, deceive and defeat any Christian he can.

How to Cancel a Guilt Trip

As long as we are ignorant of the truth, Satan will succeed. Jesus said, "You will know the truth, and the truth will set you free" (John 8:32). To cancel the guilt trips Satan would sell us, we must be students of God's truth, the Bible. There is no substitute. Whether we realize it or not, we are in a spiritual battle. God has not left us defenseless. He's given us spiritual armor and an offensive weapon in His Word ("the sword of the Spirit, which is the word of God" [Ephesians 6:17]). No wonder we struggle spiritually when we lay it aside! Think about it; no battle has ever been won defensively.

Awhile ago Charlotte and I had the opportunity to have coffee together. As our time together unfolded, so did Charlotte's story of a difficult confrontation she had made in a relationship recently. She truly felt that she had done and said the right thing. Even if her words hadn't been perfect, she knew her motive was pure. Yet since then Charlotte had struggled with a great sense of anxiety, guilt and fear.

"I know I was right in what I said," Charlotte confided. "But my friend didn't see it that way. What if I really was out of line? Should I apologize? Should I never dare to confront a friend ever again? What's more, is confrontation going to be God's role for me in my Christian walk? Personally, I don't think I can live with that!"

There were other factors that made this situation complex. Yet as we compared the facts of Charlotte's motives and behavior to God's Word, it became clear that these guilt feelings and fears were not from the Holy Spirit. As Christians we have authority over Satan through our faith in Jesus Christ. The Bible says that we can actually curtail Satan's oppression in our lives by taking a stand in faith against his harassment. As soon as Charlotte and I were aware of how she had been deceived, we prayed to reaffirm for ourselves the biblical truths we needed to claim by faith and to bind Satan from assaulting her thinking in this area.

Immediately I could sense the difference. Charlotte's countenance brightened. Clearly the burden of guilt and fear were gone. Better yet, what could have been a spiritual dead end for her was transformed through faith into a growth experience. If she ever needs to confront again, she will have this lesson to draw from. But it was knowing and applying God's Word by faith that made it all possible.

Another way Satan manipulates our guilt feelings is by selling us a checklist of unrealistic expectations. By this I mean the mental "should dos" that we tend to adopt in addition to our mental "must do" lists. It is a problem common to women the world over. In fact one therapist wrote, "Show me a woman who doesn't feel guilt, and I'll show you a man" (Lerner 1989, 187). As a rule, women tend to expect too much from themselves. And when they don't measure up, they feel guilty.

This especially seems to apply to ministry wives. In fact, unrealistic expectations and loneliness comprise the two most commonly voiced complaints shared by pastors' wives. Why? As a pastor's wife I'm tempted constantly to rush past my routine domestic responsibilities and fill my schedule with the more attractive activities that surround the church. "After all," I rationalize, "I'm the pastor's wife. I must set the example. And, besides, if I don't do it, who will?" This is all good and fine until my two worlds collide.

In our pastorate in western Washington, there was no conceivable way I could physically meet all the expectations I had for myself. The result was a continual sense of failure and guilt as both mother and ministry wife. No matter how hard I worked, it seemed I just couldn't accomplish enough to fill both roles. In time, this and additional emotional pressures combined to land me a case of classic clinical depression. By appealing to my Christian sense of self-sacrifice, Satan had duped me into burning out.

Yet it would be unfair to say I, alone, was to blame for my overcommitment to ministry. For some in the congregation had, although perhaps unknowingly, pressured me in that direction. The pastor and his wife who preceded us had been an older couple. Over the years, they had developed what apparently was a powerful, team ministry. I learned early on from some at church, how heavily involved the former pastor's wife had been in teaching and the music ministry. And it was suggested by some that I follow her example in these and other areas.

Yet my life situation was radically different than hers had been. With two small children to attend to, I simply couldn't begin to take on the ministry load she had carried. Not to mention that my talents were far different than hers.

What's more, I lacked the wealth of experience

that characterized this pastoral couple. They were seasoned in ministry, while this was our first pastorate. I was unsure of myself in this new public lifestyle. In addition, I was a new mother, and unsure about myself in that role as well. All my friends and family had been left behind when we moved to this mountain community. More than anything, I needed friendship and acceptance—not a job description.

Do you want to strengthen your pastor's effectiveness? Then reach out in love to his wife. Do what you can to compliment her, encourage her, befriend her and pray for her. Whatever you do, don't compare her with someone else. However well-meaning your criticisms may be, if they aren't couched in a relationship built on love, they could easily become misconstrued. And most ministry wives are hard enough on themselves without your added exhortation.

So is it possible to know how much "extra" to take on before you cut yourself or your family short? Yes, I believe you can. And you begin by setting priorities.

Where are you at in your life? Prayerfully consider the ministry opportunities before you. What would God have you do? Set and respond to your priorities according to Scripture.

Along with priorities comes a knowledge of your personal limitations. Your friend may be able to easily teach a Bible study, or have a family in for dinner at the drop of a hat. You may be different. Accomplishing less or in different areas is not wrong. Remember, faithfulness—not comparison or productivity—is the marker for success with God.

Finally, take time out to rest. What mom doesn't have trouble with this one? Ever notice how moms never really get sick? Somehow, they always keep going. Only hospitalization or the undertaker can seem to stop the demands that go with being a mother. So it isn't surprising that resting is probably one of my toughest battles. If I stop, I can think of a dozen things I "should be" doing. Guilt comes rolling in on my spirit like a wet fog.

But even Jesus took His disciples out of ministry to rest occasionally. I reason, if they needed to rest we can feel good in taking a break occasionally as well. Over the years, I've come to adopt a lifestyle that allows me an almost daily break away from home. My break isn't long, but I inevitably find I return refreshed and ready to pick up where I left off. And I'm coming to see the value in planning an occasional day off as well. In *Telling Yourself the Truth*, the authors remind those in ministry:

> There were times when Jesus put His own needs for rest and food ahead of ministering to others. If you try to neglect yourself and your own needs (unless you are under direct instructions from the Lord), you will court spiritual and psychological troubles. Being cruel to yourself is not necessarily holy. Jesus did your penance for you on the cross. You're free now to live in love, receiving as well as giving. (Backus and Chapian 1980, 113)

What guilt trip does Satan have you on? What

regrets, founded or otherwise, echo through your mind? Choose today to submit to God. Study your Bible. Are you truly guilty? If so, confess and forsake your sin. Follow through with restitution if God so directs. But if you discover Satan's been up to his old tricks again with you, claim God's promises and confront his lies by expressing your faith to God in prayer. It's time you learn to claim His Word and cancel your trip!

MAKING IT YOURS

1. How is guilt a "healthy" emotional response?

2. The Bible says that our natural sinfulness before God alienates us from Him. How can our relationship with God change through receiving what Christ has done? (Romans 5:8-11; 8:1-2)

3. Even as Christians, we still sin from time to time. How can we deal with the guilt of daily living? (1 John 1:9)

4. How would you define a "guilt trip"?

5. What are some ways Satan exploits our feelings to keep us from realizing God's forgiveness?

6. What are some steps you can take to overcome the false guilt brought on by unrealistic expectations?

7. Do you ever find yourself doing or not doing things in an attempt to make up for your sinfulness before God? Explain.

8. What does the Bible say about our attempts to

"make it up to God" (i.e. do penance) when we sin? (Hebrews 10:17-18)

9. How does a person experience God's acceptance and forgiveness in his or her life? (Hebrews 10:19-22, 38)

10. How much attention should be paid to guilt feelings even after known sin is confessed?

11. How can you use the Bible to defeat Satan's guilt-producing accusations? (Hebrews 4:12)

Chapter Seven

It's Never Too Late

THEY WERE OFF WITH THE CRACK of the gun, six junior high girls running with all their might for the tape in the 100-meter run. Our school had two girls in this heat. Within seconds they were pulling to a lead. Then one of our girls stumbled and fell. Incredibly, all the other girls stopped to see what had happened! I remember it all seemed like a bad dream in slow motion. As assistant coach I began yelling at our other girl, "Keep running! Don't stop running!" Somehow she heard me and again bounded away toward the tape. That day I watched the only 100-meter run I've ever seen where the winner restarted halfway through and won. Incredible! And I learned that in junior high track, anything is possible!

This same lesson came pounding home again several weeks later at league finals. April was our most talented hurdler. I remember the first day I watched her and thought with satisfaction, "There goes the league champion for sure. We've got the women's hurdle events in the bag!" However, that was before April was goofing off one Saturday and broke her arm. The doctor told us she probably wouldn't be able to do much for the rest of the season. To her credit, April continued to practice and compete, but she did poorly. So as April climbed into the blocks for the 400-meter hurdles, I wasn't expecting much. The gun went off. The girls jettisoned from their blocks. As they rounded the first curve, a change seemed to overtake April. She was running all out this time, running as never before. One after the other, she cleared hurdles with the grace of a seasoned competitor, ultimately crossing the tape in first place.

"What happened?" I asked excitedly. "You haven't done anything all season, and now you've won first place at league finals!"

"Oh, that," she said smiling. "Well, I knew if I didn't do it I'd just never be able to live with myself."

Now I can't explain how a junior high girl can stop and start in the 100-meter dash and win. Nor can I understand the rationale of a junior high girl who holds out all season for a dazzling display at league finals. I'm convinced these are some of the wonders of adolescence and thereby beyond rational comprehension. But this I do know: Too many of us accept defeat before the race of life is truly finished. Things may look bleak, but in the Christian experience it is never too late to start again.

John Mark

This was a lesson John Mark learned. If anyone

was headed toward success in his Christian experience, it was John Mark. An obscure character though he is, it is thought by some Bible scholars that it was at John Mark's home that Jesus and his disciples ate the Last Supper. Apparently he was close at hand that evening, for Mark 14:51-52 mentions "a young man, wearing nothing but a linen garment" who followed Jesus to Gethsemane. It is thought that this eyewitness was John Mark.

Later he is mentioned again. It is to John Mark's home that Peter went after his miraculous release from prison. The church was holding a prayer meeting there (Acts 12:12). Apparently John Mark's family was involved with the early church from the very outset.

Some scholars think it was Peter who led John Mark to the Lord. And Colossians 4:10 reveals that John Mark's cousin was none other than Barnabas, the church leader and one-time missionary companion of the Apostle Paul.

Indeed, it is hard to think of a better environment to develop a promising Christian leader. John Mark had all the advantages for success in his Christian walk. Still, John Mark began his walk with the Lord in failure.

Barnabas and Paul had just delivered a financial gift to the Christians in Judea and returned to Antioch. There they were officially commissioned as missionaries to the Gentiles. Later, when they left Antioch and headed to Asia Minor, they took John Mark with them (Acts 12:25-13:5).

The three men traveled together until Paul confronted a sorcerer who was interfering with Paul's presentation of the gospel. Empowered by the Holy Spirit, Paul rebuked the sorcerer and cursed him with blindness. The Bible says, "Immediately mist and darkness came over him [the sorcerer], and he groped about, seeking someone to lead him by the hand" (13:11). The man to whom Paul was witnessing immediately received Christ, but another reaction was set off in the heart of John Mark.

We are really never told why he decided to leave the mission field. Perhaps the spiritual warfare he had just witnessed was more than he had bargained for. Perhaps it was the hardships of ministry, loneliness or word of problems at home. Whatever the reason, John Mark soon packed up his things and left. The parting was a bitter one. Barnabas stayed with Paul. Yet, much later they argued so bitterly about John Mark's desertion that the two men stopped ministering together (15:36-40). Barnabas took John Mark and returned to Cyprus. Paul chose Silas as a traveling companion and headed for Syria.

Although much of John Mark's life is shrouded in mystery, apparently somewhere along the way confidence was reborn. The promising young missionary who had failed so miserably began again and this time succeeded. Second Timothy 4:11 is a beautiful commendation by the once bitter Apostle Paul. He wrote: "Get Mark and bring him with you, because he is helpful to me in my ministry." The young man Paul had once thought untrustworthy was now sought specifically by the imprisoned apostle. The one who brought such discord and disappointment was now described as "helpful." John Mark had changed.

It's Never Too Late with God

It's never too late to start afresh with God. Jill Briscoe in her book, *By Hook or by Crook*, writes:

> Jesus wants us to know He will give us the freedom to fail and also the faith to pick ourselves up, dust ourselves off, and try again. And this will probably go on until eventually we see Him as He is and be like Him (1 John 3:2). (Briscoe 1987, 107)

What a gift this "freedom to fail" is! It is a freedom that grants faith in the God of the impossible. Indeed, not everything is possible with man, "but with God all things are possible" (Matthew 19:26). By faith in God, the believer finds the courage to try again. Applied to our lives, this kind of faith can work miracles. Jesus said, "I tell you the truth, if you have faith as small as a mustard seed, you can say to this mountain, 'Move from here to there' and it will move. Nothing will be impossible for you" (17:21).

Joe experienced such a miracle in his life. For over 20 years Joe had been captive to drug addiction. Finally difficulties in his family, with work and the burden of addiction itself broke Joe's resistance to God. One day he walked into a church, heard the gospel and gave his shattered life to Christ. When he walked into my husband's office about a week later, he was just beginning the torment of withdrawal. Was it even possible for a lifetime addict to leave his addiction behind? I don't think either Joe or my husband and I were really sure. By his own admission he had tried to free himself before. It had never worked. In the end the craving for drugs always won. Yet this time, by God's grace, Joe was set free from his addiction. Even the withdrawal symptoms had hardly been noticeable. God had worked a miracle. It's never too late with God.

Seth and Melinda discovered the same to be true for their marriage. Both seemed to be strong Christians. Both were actively involved in a fundamental church. You would never have thought that unresolved problems were undermining their lives at home. Yet as all secret illnesses go, their problems festered until Melinda was unfaithful. Seth was devastated. Feelings of anger, hurt and distrust waged war in his heart. The number of times he was tempted to simply walk away were beyond counting. Still, Seth stayed. Melinda broke off the adulterous relationship she had become enmeshed in, and together they sought counseling. Step by step they began rebuilding their marriage. It wasn't easy. Indeed, leaving often seemed the less painful way out. But by God's grace they were determined to see this relationship work. God rewarded their faith. Today their marriage is stronger than ever before. Both husband and wife are again active in their local church, being powerfully used of God to win the lost to Him.

Could it be that if it wasn't too late for John Mark, Seth and Melinda, or Joe, that it is neither too late for you and the failures you face in your life? Setbacks and discouragements are always part of life. But they do not need to be the final word.

Does this mean that we should never be discouraged? Is discouragement a sin? Does it mean we never surrender a battle, even when the evidence seems overwhelmingly against us?

Dealing with Discouragement

While in college I took a rock climbing class. It was an easy physical education credit until the day we faced our first climb, a 150-foot boulder in Joshua Tree National Monument. Fortunately an experienced climber went ahead, anchoring the rope at key points along the way. Not that I could just climb up the rope. The idea in climbing is to use your fingers, feet, sometimes anything, to secure a handhold or foothold and scale the face on your own strength. The rope is simply to break your fall should a handhold fail. That day as I experienced my first climb, I learned how important good handholds were. Gazing down from 80 feet or so, I realized just one slip and I could be history. Believe me, I made the most of every move from that point on.

Life, in some ways, parallels climbing. At times life seems incredibly rough. Some days it seems to take all you have to just hold on. And sometimes the handholds you thought were secure seem to be dribbling away like sand between your fingers. Discouragement blankets your soul. You feel like giving up. Perhaps you wonder secretly if you can even go on.

Have you ever felt that way? Who hasn't felt like giving up at one time or another? Discouragement is a universal experience. Life is a balance—emotionally up times are leveled out with emotionally down times. So you aren't failing as a Christian if you find yourself discouraged from time to time. But if we wallow in our discouragement, Satan can break our concentration on life's climb, we can loose our handholds and plummet into depression. A wise climber knows the anchors he can set in the rock to give himself an extra edge. I believe God has given us a similar set of anchors for dealing with discouragement.

Of course, there are many reasons a person feels discouraged. Some causes are biological, chemical or hormonal changes within your body. Sometimes discouragement comes as a result of physical or emotional exhaustion. This was Elijah's experience after God's great victory over the prophets of Baal on Mount Carmel (1 Kings 18:19). That day after leading the contest of God against Baal, slaying 450 idolatrous prophets and then lifting the plague of drought affecting Israel, Elijah was still energized enough to outrun King Ahab's chariot. Is it any surprise that in the next chapter he collapses under a broom tree in the desert and begs to die (19:4)? The poor guy was simply worn out!

You may find a similar pattern is true for you. We don't have to do all Elijah did to feel tired. My husband and I have learned that Sunday afternoons are a bad time to evaluate our ministry. After the busyness of our morning at church, we are simply too tired. Evaluations attempted on Sunday afternoon inevitably lead to discouragement. By waiting until the next day, we are able to recover emotionally enough to be more objective and able to handle criticism.

What is the weak spot in your schedule? Are there changes you can make so you don't set yourself up for an emotional backlash simply because you are too tired?

More often though, prolonged discouragement has mental causes. In ministry it is often the loss of expectations that discourage. Jeremiah struggled with such discouragement. In Jeremiah 15:16-18 he complained:

> When your words came, I ate them;
>   they were my joy and my heart's delight,
> for I bear your name,
>   O LORD God Almighty.
> I never sat in the company of revelers,
>   never made merry with them;
> I sat alone because your hand was on me
>   and you had filled me with indignation.
> Why is my pain unending
>   and my wound grievous and incurable?
> Will you be to me like a deceptive brook,
>   like a spring that fails?

Elijah had a similar response. He said,

> I have been very zealous for the LORD God Almighty. The Israelites have rejected your covenant, broken down your altars, and put your prophets to death with the sword. I am the only one left, and now they are trying to kill me too. (1 Kings 19:10)

Both men were struggling with a sense of loss. Jeremiah had interceded faithfully for his people, only to be told that God was intent on judging them

(Jeremiah 14:11-12; 15:1). God told Jeremiah he was no longer to intercede, but prophesy God's coming judgment. It was a hard, lonely assignment, and the patriot heart of Jeremiah rebelled. He cried, "Alas, my mother, that you gave me birth, a man with whom the whole land strives and contends! I have neither lent nor borrowed, yet everyone curses me" (15:10). Heartache for his people, disappointment in God's mercy and his own loneliness combined to plummet this prophet to the lowest point in his ministry (Jensen 1966, 53).

Elijah's complaint is somewhat similar. Ministry had been lonelier than perhaps he had anticipated. Now he was afraid he had lost God's protection as well. This mental combination (along with his physical/emotional exhaustion) spelled not only discouragement for Elijah, but depression as well.

Can you relate to these two pastors? Life just doesn't seem fair at times, does it? When life really isn't fair, and we're the losers, it's only natural to experience a sense of loss. Whether our disappointment turns to discouragement, and discouragement to depression, depends a great deal on our spiritual handholds. If our faith is anchored in God, no disappointment, no matter how great, has to be the end.

Spiritual Handholds

One such handhold is being honest with God. Both Jeremiah and Elijah prayed honest, discouraged prayers. In Psalm 42:3-4 David prays: "My tears have been my food day and night, while men say to me all day long, 'Where is your God?' These things I remember as I pour out my soul. . . ."

So go ahead and weep. Pour out your disappointments before the throne of God. God already knows how you feel, He's just waiting for your heartache to lead you to Him.

Another handhold is to rediscover God's call on your life. Elijah just wanted to stop everything— ministry, the threats he faced, even life itself. He wanted to quit. God came in a still, small voice and recommissioned him for service. It almost doesn't seem fair. Elijah was worn out. If anything, he deserved early retirement. But that is the crux of the matter. It is not our place to decide when we are finished. We are here to serve Him. When we lose sight of that, we are serving no one but ourselves. This is why God rebuked Jeremiah's discouraged prayer. God said, "If you repent, I will restore you that you may serve me; if you utter worthy, not worthless words, you will be my spokesman" (Jeremiah 15:19). Jeremiah's failure was not in his honesty before God, but in the accompanying decision to resist God's call on his life.

What is it that God has called you to do? Has God called you to be a missionary, a ministry wife, a mother, a pastor? Renew your commitment to obey His calling. You probably won't feel like it, but that's where faith comes in, doesn't it?

One gray dawn I rediscovered these three hand-holds. I was on my way to lead a newly organized ministry wives' support group. We had been meeting for several months now. But although I had worked hard to promote this ministry, attendance had been small. I was tempted to be discouraged.

I could call and cancel, I thought. *Probably only one or two women will go. And besides, there are countless other jobs at home I could be doing.* But then I had to admit that any new ministry grows slowly at first. It was too soon to give up. No, I had to see this through for another month anyway.

As I headed north along the highway, I continued to voice my discouragement in prayer. "I don't know, Lord," I prayed. "I truly believe there's a need for ministry wives to meet together for mutual support and encouragement. I know such a group would have been invaluable to me during our first pastorate. But the attendance seems so low. Maybe I'm just believing in a need that doesn't exist."

As expected, the turnout was small. But the sharing and fellowship with ministry sisters that morning was exceptionally sweet. I was soon glad I came. Then as we prepared to close our session in prayer, Debra's secret heartache surfaced. Debra and her husband, Mike, were being heavily criticized by the governing board of their church. In addition, several families they had worked so hard to draw into the church had recently quit attending. "We're just not sure what to do," she confessed quietly. "Maybe the time has come for us to move on."

My heart went out to her. I could empathize with their discouragement: the long hours, the unseen sacrifices, the hopes and disappointment that her few words reflected. As our group held hands around the table that day and prayed for Debra and Mike, I could sense an outpouring of God's love. I could also hear God speaking to my discouraged soul. "See," He whispered softly, "there really is a need for this ministry. I haven't led you astray. Take heart. I'm in this."

It would have been so easy to cancel out that morning and stay at home. But what a blessing I would have missed! And needed encouragement to a hurting ministry couple would have gone unspoken. Instead, hanging onto the handholds of honest prayer, a commitment to God's calling and a sensitivity to God's presence had replaced discouragement with rejoicing.

So in your discouragement, grab hold of God's call. He has a plan for you and hasn't forsaken you. In fact, God's continuing presence is another handhold for surviving discouragement.

God has promised never to desert His children (Hebrews 13:5). No matter how discouraged you are, no matter how distant God may seem, God is still present and taking your part. Satan would love to see you ground to hopelessness by your discouragement. Yet God desires otherwise. When all else fails, He's there to see you through. God's presence is an anchor proved sufficient for any of life's storms.

When You Just Can't Beat "The Blues"

You may protest that you've tried all these things (and more, perhaps), yet still you struggle with discouragement. Take one last look at the struggle of Elijah. He may have conquered Baal worship and run down Mount Carmel all in a day, but the recovery process took much longer. The trip to Mount Horeb alone took 40 days! Then once he arrived, Elijah still wasn't ready to listen to God. One would think a wind strong enough to shatter rocks would shake Elijah up and cause him to remember the mighty God that was on his side (1 Kings 19:11). It didn't. Next came a bone-jarring earthquake. I've experienced a few small earthquakes. They always made me feel closer to God; yet Elijah was still depressed. Then a fire roared across the mountain. And after the fire, God's voice came in a gentle whisper (19:12-13).

Elijah's words betray not only faulty thinking, but a sense of deep loneliness. This is often the experience of a depressed person. God answered Elijah in two interesting ways. First, Elijah is reminded by this encounter of God's abiding presence on his behalf. Second, God provided a friend. The anointing of Elisha to be Elijah's successor was the last instruction of the Lord (19:16). Yet it was the first instruction Elijah hurried to carry out (19:19-21). No doubt the purpose of this friendship was twofold: that Elisha be trained as a prophet, and that Elijah have the emotional support of companionship.

Elijah's experience highlights two additional lessons about discouragement. First, it takes time to recover. If you are struggling, give yourself the time to heal. Even the great Elijah didn't bounce back the next day. Second, we recover faster when we don't alienate ourselves from others. Ecclesiastes shares this insight:

> Two are better than one,
>   because they have a good return for
>   their work:
> If one falls down,
>   his friend can help him up.

> But pity the man who falls
> and has no one to help him up!
> Though one may be overpowered,
> two can defend themselves.
> A cord of three strands is not quickly broken.
> (4:9-10,12)

How often we foolishly hold ourselves above close friendships. This is particularly true for pastors' wives. Somehow as ministry wives, we feel we must be everyone's friend equally. I felt that way when we first entered the ministry. I felt I didn't have the right to nurture close friendships; especially not within the church. The result was that while I seemed outgoing, I soon became terribly lonely. And the lonelier I felt, the more difficult heartfelt ministry became.

Fortunately, I eventually began to risk asking Mary to pray for me. She seemed to be a sensitive and discreet person. Still, I never imagined she'd become a trusted friend. With her two children already grown and gone, our lives seemed too different to be brought close. But Mary was God's choice in a friend for me. In the years that have passed since those first tentative requests, our friendship has continued to grow. Through her prayers, I've found the strength to: face a difficult move to the midwest and back; the courage to face personal hardship; and the vision to pursue a ministry to pastors' wives. And there have been other friends, as well, who have likewise shaped my life and ministry. Looking back, I simply can't imagine returning to the shallow, ineffective ministry I had as a lonely pastor's wife. Close friendships are important no matter who you are.

Don't neglect the rich encouragement God has given you in relationships. Time enjoyed with godly friends is time well spent.

Satan's Garage Sale

The story is told that Satan once had a garage sale. On a table before him was spread an odd assortment of tools: anger, jealousy, fear, etc. Among them was one very dilapidated tool. In fact, it was so worn that it appeared hardly usable. A curious visitor picked it up. "How much do you want for this?" he asked half in jest. "Oh that," Satan answered, "I've decided not to sell that. That's *discouragement*, and I use that more than any of the others. No, I could never get by without that."

Have you been allowing Satan to steal your hope? Don't let him fool you. In God's kingdom it's never too late to start afresh. Oh, the realities of life may block us in some of our aspirations. But God's call to faithful obedience is ever timely. I have a button that reads "My Future's So Bright I Need Sun Glasses." It sounds rather cocky, but for Christians such optimism is fact. Because of Christ, the future belongs to us. Truly it's never too late.

MAKING IT YOURS

1. How does John Mark's life illustrate it is never too late to start afresh with God?

2. Does the ability to start again mean we should never be discouraged?

3. Is discouragement sin? Is it wrong to surrender a battle, even when the evidence seems overwhelmingly against us?

4. There are many reasons why a person feels discouraged or depressed. For example, some medications will make a person feel somewhat depressed. See if you can list three additional causes for discouragement.

5. How might Elijah's ministry load in chapter 18 have set him up for an emotional backlash in chapter 19? (1 Kings 18:20-19:8)

6. Discouragement can come from a sense of loss. How did Jeremiah's hope for Judah differ from God's plan? (Jeremiah 14:11, 19-22; 15:1-4)

7. Honesty and intimacy go hand-in-hand. But does this apply to our discouraged prayers as well? Do you think emotional honesty in our prayers can help lift the cloud of discouragement? Compare the discouraged prayers of Jeremiah and Elijah. (Jeremiah 15:16-18; 1 Kings 19:10)

8. What is one way God responded to Elijah's discouragement? (1 Kings 19:15-17)

9. Why is it wrong to decide when we want to "retire" from serving God?

10. What promise does God give to His children that is a special comfort at times of discouragement? (Hebrews 13:5b)

11. A deep sense of loneliness is often the experi-

ence of the depressed person. God partly
answered Elijah's struggle with depression by
providing a friend in Elisha. Read Ecclesiastes
4:9-12. How are friendships a gift from God,
especially in times of discouragement?

Chapter Eight

The Case of Mistaken Identity

SCOTT KNOCKED LOUDLY ON THE front door for the second time. He was the police and fire department chaplain for our community. This afternoon he was responding to a woman's suicide threat. Because it was from a woman in crisis, he'd asked me to come along.

"What do we do if no one answers?" I asked nervously. Distraught screams from inside assured me we weren't too late—at least not yet. Before Scott could answer my question, the door opened. A small boy let us in; his eyes were wide in fear. "She's in there," he said pointing to the kitchen.

The scene that greeted us was unbelievable. Dirty laundry was heaped on the table and floor. Opened cans of food and dirty dishes filled the kitchen sink, spilling across the countertop. In the middle of the room sat a frail, unkempt, young mother, her head in her hands, rocking and moaning. In the next two hours that we spent with her, one message kept ringing out repeatedly: "I'm no good! I'm just a lot of garbage. I wish I could die. I'm just no good!"

It was a false message of course. But for the moment, drugs, alcohol and personal problems had made it the only message she could hear. Yet interestingly, poor self-esteem messages similar to this one are a problem for nearly everyone—especially women. In his book *Hide Or Seek*, Dr. James Dobson shares research indicating that low self-esteem is the leading cause of depression in American women today. He writes: "The conclusion . . . is inescapable: inferiority and inadequacy have become constant companions of many, perhaps most, American women" ([1974] 1979, 143).

Why are these low self-esteem messages so pervasive? Low self-esteem plagues our society because we foolishly play comparison games. We are a nation of competitors, always striving to be one up on those around us. Whether it is beauty, intelligence or achievement, we chase after self improvement like a cat chasing its tail. And, since we've tied self-esteem to some vague standard of accomplishment in these areas, we dare not give up pursuit. For many, denial of personal limitations is less painful than the acceptance of reality. Still, acceptance is inevitable for all of us. Beauty fades; the intellect looses its edge; even outstanding achievements soon ring empty or are forgotten. The chase for the impossible dream of esteem based on standards of comparison comes crashing down around our ears and depression follows. It's not surprising. Dorothy Corkille Briggs, in her book *Your Child's Self-Esteem*, writes:

"Low self-esteem is tied to *impossible* demands on the self" (1970, 39). Indeed, success by comparison is just that—impossible!

Fortunately, God doesn't measure our self-esteem on a public graph. His acceptance is personal and intimate. No one knows us better than He does. God knows our limitations, our strengths and the dreams we can grow toward. Because of its perfect completeness, God's individual plan for each one of us is really the only reasonable basis for self-esteem. But first let's look briefly at the three arenas of competition mentioned earlier.

Self-Esteem Tied to Beauty

Physical attractiveness has long been an important battlefield for self-esteem. This is especially true for women. Men are freer to win self-esteem through their intellectual prowess or career achievement. Culturally women have been held back from competing in these areas. Besides, "the reason the average woman would rather have beauty than brains is because she knows the average man can see better than he can think" (Dobson [1974] 1979, 52).

Still, physical attractiveness is socially important to both sexes. We see this in David's boyhood anointing as king of Israel. In First Samuel 16:1 God commissions the prophet/priest Samuel to visit Jesse in Bethlehem and anoint one of his sons to take the throne following Saul's reign. The mission seemed simple enough, except that Jesse had eight sons! Which one should he anoint? As Samuel looked at the faces around him, his eyes stopped on Eliab. Eliab was the eldest, no doubt nearly a man. Surely this must be the one God intended. As

Samuel considered Eliab, God spoke to his heart:

> Do not consider his appearance or his height, for I have rejected him. The LORD does not look at the things man looks at. Man looks at the outward appearance, but the LORD looks at the heart. (16:7)

Samuel went on to consider the next brother. In fact, six more brothers would pass before Samuel and be rejected before God would reveal His choice. God's choice was David, the youngest, deemed so unimportant that he was still out in the fields tending sheep.

Interestingly, when David arrived, it was his appearance that Samuel first recorded. He described David as "ruddy, with a fine appearance and handsome features" (16:12). Beauty is important to mankind. Yet God's judgment is based on a standard apart from human comparison. Because of His omniscient plan for David, God instructed Samuel, "Rise and anoint him; he is the one" (16:12).

Peter addressed women in their concern for physical attractiveness. In First Peter 3:3-4 he wrote:

> Your beauty should not come from outward adornment, such as braided hair and the wearing of gold jewelry and fine clothes. Instead, it should be that of your inner self, the unfading beauty of a gentle and quiet spirit, which is of great worth in God's sight.

Does this mean we should just ignore our outward

appearance? Certainly not; physical neglect is no credit to the gospel! What Peter meant is that we should not neglect the inner self by focusing exclusively on the outward self.

Self-Esteem Tied to Intelligence

"When the birth of a first-born child is imminent, his parents pray that he will be normal—that is, 'average.' But from that moment on, average will not be good enough" (Dobson [1974] 1979, 43).

Intelligence—the second arena in the battle for self-esteem. Did you know that there is even a sperm bank in California supplied by highly intelligent men for parents desiring a child genetically predisposed to a higher I.Q.? Ridiculous isn't it—or is it? We assume that intelligence will earn respect, a higher income and self-esteem. What's more, it's a multiple win. The child wins prestige and the parents share in its glow. Or did you think those honor roll bumper stickers that read "My Son/Daughter Is An Honor Roll Student" are for the child's benefit only? Yet God says intelligence isn't everything. In fact, Paul writes:

> For the foolishness of God is wiser than man's wisdom, and the weakness of God is stronger than man's strength. . . .
> But God chose the foolish things of the world to shame the wise; God chose the weak things of the world to shame the strong. He chose the lowly things of this world and the despised things—and the things that are not—to nullify the things that are so that no one may boast before him. (1 Corinthians 1:25-29)

The things of God are simple. In fact, they are so simple that the world regards them as foolish. Accordingly, many worldly wise men and women have missed out on life with God. The gospel seems too simple—too good to be true.

Perhaps the gospel seems too humbling as well. After all, *anyone* can receive salvation by faith. It's so easy, so complete, that God's plan leaves no room for boasting in personal achievement. Yet isn't that the beauty of God's way? His truth is available to all. As someone said, "He puts the cookies on the lower shelf where we can reach them." Further, God has given each believer a private tutor in the Holy Spirit. The Bible says: "But when he, the Spirit of truth, comes, he will guide you into all truth" (John 16:13). The spiritual realities of Christianity are there for each and every believer desiring to investigate.

You see, God wants us to be His success stories. He wants the world to look at our lives and wonder at the difference He's made. God delights to build His kingdom through common people like you and me.

When I was first introduced to Ted, I hardly bothered to remember his name. Ted—no doubt, like others you've met—seemed such an ordinary, almost boring, person. Neither his physical appearance nor his personality seemed to offer much worth remembering. But after two years fellowshipping with Ted, he's become a brother in the Lord I'll never forget. What made the difference?

The difference came as I watched Ted in action. For Christ had transformed this ordinary man into a soul-winning dynamo. He passionately loved the lost people around him, taking every opportunity to share the gospel. As a result, many listened and gave their hearts to Christ.

Ted could have allowed self-consciousness to bar his way. He didn't. He could have been intimidated by another's prestige or intellect. But it was their souls, not their I.Q., that was on Ted's heart. In fact, Ted has admittedly lost count of all the individuals he's led to Christ. "It really doesn't matter how many," he told me one day. "It's that they come to Christ. That's the important thing to me. And I'm just glad I can have a part in that."

Intelligence is a worthwhile pursuit. The Proverbs urge us forward in the pursuit of wisdom, extolling it above material treasure (Proverbs 8:10–11). Learning (especially applied learning—wisdom) is certainly valuable to our own quality of life and those whose lives we touch. Still, the lesson is clear. It's not your "smarts" that matter so much to God, as your "heart" attitude. It's the humble person, like Ted, that God wants to use to change the world.

Self-Esteem Tied to Achievement

Bronze statues stand proudly above several traffic islands in the city where I grew up. One was some soldier whose name and reputation I can never remember. I've often wondered how many people bother reflecting on his import commemorated there. For, as far as I could tell, he seemed basically unnoticed, except by the pigeons that used him for a perch. Fame is so fleeting. Even the most accomplished are forgotten within a decade or two. Why is it, then, that we strive so hard to distinguish ourselves with honors or possessions?

Paul was a man of many honors. Through his intense training in Judaism, he had risen through the ranks to the very top. His conversion to Christianity changed all that. Instead of being sought out for honor, he was despised as a follower of Jesus Christ. Did this shake Paul's sense of self-esteem? Not in the least. Philippians 3:4–9 says:

> If anyone else thinks he has reasons to put confidence in the flesh, I have more: circumcised on the eighth day, of the people of Israel, of the tribe of Benjamin, a Hebrew of Hebrews; in regard to the law, a Pharisee; as for zeal, persecuting the church; as for legalistic righteousness, faultless.
>
> But whatever was to my profit I now consider loss for the sake of Christ. What is more, I consider everything a loss compared to the surpassing greatness of knowing Christ Jesus my Lord.

What we value so much in this world matters little to God. Where do you draw your sense of self-esteem? Beauty, intellect and achievement—these are the world's building blocks. Yet as we've seen, they all crumble eventually. Those who try to build their lives upon them are headed for sure disappointment. So just how does someone draw his or her sense of esteem from a private relationship with Jesus Christ?

Building Self-Esteem that Lasts

Turn with me back to the dawn of human history. For it is here that we find the first building block of godly esteem. In five days God created the order of the universe. The plants, the animals, the countless stars and galaxies—everything was in place except man. On the sixth day God created him. He said: "Let us make man in our image, in our likeness, and let them rule over the fish of the sea and the birds of the air, over the livestock, over all the earth, and over all the creatures that move along the ground" (Genesis 1:26). The record continues, "So God created man in his own image, in the image of God he created him; male and female he created them" (1:27).

The imprint of God's image is mentioned four times in these two verses. The import of this statement is inescapable. From the least impressive to the most mighty, we all bear the image of God!

Sin has marred this image by separating us from our heritage in God, but when a person receives Christ, all of that is restored. In addition, we are granted total acceptance before God the Father. Accordingly, Christians should have the best esteem of any people group on the planet! For we not only bear God's image, we are the children of God as well.

Do you remember the children's tale *The Ugly Duckling*? One spring, in a nest among the rushes, a brood of ducklings was born. Small, awkward, little balls of fluff, they tumbled after their proud mother as she paraded around the marsh graciously receiving compliments from the other animals on her fine family. There was only one flaw. The youngest duckling was terribly ugly! So while the other ducklings found praise and welcome, his life was defined by mockery and rejection. At last even his mother said she wished he had never been born. Poor thing! The pain and loneliness of a broken heart thrust him out into the world. But that too held only a grudging and bitter acceptance. By the following spring he had become so depressed that he rushed out to greet some returning swans, imploring them to kill him. Of course, it was at that moment he caught his reflection in the water and realized he wasn't a duck at all, but instead a beautiful swan. The tragedy of his life hadn't been his former ugliness, but believing in a mistaken identity. (Andersen 1955)

I think this tale has a lesson for us all: our inner identity is more important than our outer appearance. If we struggle with our self-worth, it is only because our information is incomplete. We are the friends of God (John 15:13-15). We are His children (1:12), chosen and adopted by a loving Heavenly Father (Romans 8:15) and given a share in the inheritance of Christ Himself (8:17)! What's more, God has entrusted to us the immeasurable honor of representing Him before the world (2 Corinthians 5:20).

Are you discouraged about your physical appearance? The Christian is clothed in the perfect righteousness of God. Do you struggle with feeling inferior in your intellect? The Bible says, "The knowledge of the secrets of the kingdom of heaven has been given to you" (Matthew 13:11). Are you seeking achievement? What greater honor than to have a part in building the supreme and only lasting kingdom in the universe—the kingdom of God (Hebrews 12:28)! Yes, if Christians struggle with low self-esteem, it is only because they've lost sight of their incredible identity in Christ.

And all this is provided from a heart of love. For it was God's love that brought Christ to Calvary. John 3:16 says, "God so loved the world that he gave his one and only Son, that whoever believes in him shall not perish but have eternal life." This is not a condescending sacrifice of pity. It has been God's plan from the beginning that we bear His image, enjoying unbroken fellowship with Him. Sin got in the way and marred all that. Yet God's love is greater—love greater than all our sin. Consider these words: "This is love: not that we loved God, but that he loved us and sent his Son as an atoning sacrifice for our sins. Dear friends, since God so loved us, we also ought to love one another" (1 John 4:10-11). God cherishes you! Do you cherish yourself? We are instructed to "love one another." Certainly that command must start in our own lives.

About Accepting Handicaps

Perhaps you protest. *That's easy for you to say,* you think to yourself, *but you don't have to live with this!* You are wrong. We all face handicaps (inward or outward) of one type or another. Some handicaps are easier to conceal, but none of us is perfect. Still, it is true that for many, God's creation falls short of the false standards of perfection that our society has erected.

Perhaps that is why God often chose handicapped men to transform into His foremost leaders—look at Moses. What a great man of God he was. Leading difficult Israel through the Red Sea and trials of the wilderness. Yet Moses started his career hiding from society, consumed with feelings of inferiority.

Moses was shepherding his father-in-law's flock one day when he saw the most amazing sight—a bush that was on fire, but wasn't being consumed. Moses walked over to take a better look. As he approached God called to him from the bush.

> "Moses! Moses!"
> And Moses said, "Here I am."
> "I have indeed seen the misery of my people in Egypt. I have heard them crying out because of their slave drivers. . . . So now, go. I am sending you to Pharaoh to bring my people the Israelites out of Egypt." (Exodus 3:4, 7, 10)

Moses resisted God's call. One after another he found excuses why he was the wrong man for the job. One by one God answered his excuses, promising Moses His presence and enabling. Finally Moses shared his core fear. "O LORD, I have never been eloquent, neither in the past nor since you have spoken to your servant. I am slow of speech and tongue" (4:10). Moses may have considered himself handicapped. He may have thought he was lacking in mental capacity or perhaps he simply struggled with a speech impediment. In either case, leading the fledgling nation Israel was beyond his wildest dreams. No, he was far more content to remain a shepherd in the silences of the desert barrens.

God wasn't satisfied with Moses' attitude, however. "The LORD said to him, 'Who gave man his mouth? Who makes him deaf or mute? Who gives him sight or makes him blind? Is it not I, the LORD?

Now go; I will help you speak and will teach you what to say' " (4:11).

It is true that Moses continued to resist God's call. God reluctantly granted him Aaron (his brother) to be his spokesman. Yet through the years, God transformed this unlikely shepherd into one of the greatest leaders of Israel's history. By Exodus 18 Moses is respected as the leading judge over private disputes. The people came and presented their cases before him, listening to his decisions. It hardly sounds like the same Moses, does it? It wasn't. God had transformed a shepherd of sheep into a shepherd of men. In fact the lengthy book of Deuteronomy is basically three sermons delivered by Moses (the "slow of speech and tongue") to the nation of Israel.

Yet Moses' story isn't that unique, for God delights to show Himself strong in our weaknesses. Paul said, "I will boast all the more gladly about my weaknesses, so that Christ's power may rest on me. . . . For when I am weak, then I am strong" (2 Corinthians 12:9-10). And he spoke in reference to a handicap in his life as well.

I learned a poignant lesson on self-esteem one August at an elite women's basketball camp. Girls had come from across the Northwest to train for a week under expert coaches. At the opening session, the professional staff was introduced. But one could almost hear the gasp of revulsion and unbelief as Jim stepped forward. Jim was handicapped. Birth defects had disfigured his face. Several fingers on both hands were fused together. Indeed, his hands looked more like a matched set of pincers rather than fingers. And Jim wasn't on staff to coach—he was there to deal with injuries.

But through Christ, Jim had come to accept his handicaps. As the week progressed, I watched Jim kneel and gently and expertly attend to one injury after another. Those who started the week avoiding Jim, softened their attitude to acceptance. Eventually Jim's companionship became a coveted commodity, leaving him with hardly a moment to himself.

The week was ended with a sharing time. I was touched by the many young women who had not only sharpened their athletic skills, but admittedly deepened their relationship with God. But tears filled my eyes, as one after another thanked Jim for the specific impact he had been on their lives. And when the girls gave him a standing ovation, there wasn't a dry eye in the place.

What are your shortcomings? Do you dread them? You needn't. Shortcomings are not anchors in our lives. For when we yield our handicaps to God, they become the window of our soul, conveying Christ's light to a weary world.

Learning to Cherish Ourselves

One final thought regarding self-esteem: cherish yourself. Can you imagine working for a boss who never gave you a day off? Yet sometimes we act in such a way toward ourselves. One expert on this subject wrote:

> Do I treat myself with respect? Or do I play the game of running myself down? Do I sometimes take a trip, buy something, or give myself

a little indulgence? . . . Do I respect my body's physical and emotional requirements and do I actively try to meet them? Do I carve out blocks of time to spend with others who enjoy me? Do I save time for doing things I like? (Remember: the more fulfilled you are, the more you nurture others.) (Briggs 1970, 93-94)

A complete break from home may not be possible for everyone. But what about a 30-minute walk, or scheduling lunch with a friend once in awhile? I generally take 20 to 30 minutes to go jogging every day. It has become a break from the noise and demands of home that I genuinely look forward to. What ways can you think of to cherish yourself? At the very least, you should find and protect some time daily for Bible reading and prayer. This isn't indulgence; it's a basic need. (If you still feel guilty, remember that personal devotions are also an excellent example to set before your family. They need to see you protect this time, as much as you need it yourself.) Whatever ideas you come up with, talk them over with your husband or a supportive friend and start actively loving yourself. After all, if you don't give yourself a break, who will?

Making Changes

Satan would like to keep every believer mired in the pain and paralysis of low self-esteem. If we can believe statistics, he's been very effective at doing just that. But you needn't give him the upper hand in your life any longer. Reject the false standards of perfection that the world holds up. Decide instead to deepen your relationship with the loving God who created you who created you and has tailor-made aspirations for your life (Jeremiah 29:11). Reject the temptation to try and build esteem by comparing yourself to others. Determine, by God's grace, to develop your strengths and surrender your weaknesses to Him. Thank Him for the handicaps He's given you. It's attitudes like these that will truly change your life. Reprogramming your thoughts to focus on God gives hope, acceptance, peace, joy and—in the end—beauty. Not beauty according to the world's ever fluctuating concepts, but a quiet beauty of the heart that is a treasure to its owner and the envy of the world.

MAKING IT YOURS

1. What are three arenas in which society competes to establish self-esteem?

2. What is more important to God than our outward appearance? (1 Samuel 16:7; 1 Peter 3:3-4)

3. Describe the balance between inner and outer-beauty that the Bible teaches. (1 Corinthians 6:19-20; 1 Timothy 4:7-8)

4. Is intelligence a worthwhile pursuit? Why or why not? (Proverbs 8:10-11; 23:12)

5. How does the gospel (and its impact on lives) stand in opposition to society's emphasis on personal intelligence? (1 Corinthians 1:25-29)

6. What does Paul's attitude toward his achievements tell us about using achievements as the

basis for measuring self-worth? (Philippians 3:4-9)

7. In what way was man's creation unique? (Genesis 1:26-27)

8. Read the following verses. Because of Christ, what is our true identity before God?
   • John 1:12
   • John 15:13-15
   • Romans 8:15
   • Romans 8:17
   • 2 Corinthians 5:20

9. What motivated God to provide such a rich identity for us? (1 John 4:9-10)

10. If God has loved us in this way, how are we to treat ourselves? (1 John 4:11)

11. What about handicaps? Why might a perfect Creator allow handicaps or deformities? (2 Corinthians 12:7-10; Exodus 4:10-12)

Chapter Nine

What You Sow Is What You Reap

HE WAS JUST A BOY. In his hands was a simple meal—two fish and five small, flat, barley cakes—hardly fare to feed over 5,000. Yet when he offered it to Jesus, that's exactly what happened. Taking the cakes and fish, Jesus gave thanks, broke them in pieces and gave them to the disciples. A miracle followed as the meal was multiplied. Just when the disciples feared the food would run out, more bread and fish appeared, until finally all had been served. And when they collected the scraps, the broken pieces filled 12 baskets! It was the only meal in history where the leftovers were greater than the original entree! And why was this? Because a small boy placed what he had in the Master's hands (John 6:1-13).

In the book of Daniel, we read about a party thrown by King Belshazzar. He didn't have near the crowd to feed that Jesus did (only a thousand guests

125

in attendance), but he did his best to entertain. You can imagine however, that the fare was far more sumptuous than barley cakes and fish. This was a royal feast. Wine flowed in abundance. Only one thing could improve the evening—an ironic, ethnic jest against the Jews. Belshazzar ordered that the sacred gold and silver goblets be brought. These were the goblets taken from the temple when Babylon, during the reign of King Nebuchadnezzar, captured Jerusalem. Not only were they valuable, but they were known to be holy as well. King Nebuchadnezzar (who had learned to fear God through his lapse into mental illness) had wisely set them aside in his treasury. But Belshazzar had yet to learn his father's lesson of humility. The Hebrew God meant nothing to him. After all, He had not protected the Jews from captivity, had He? Wine-filled goblets were raised around the room in a chorus of toasts to the plethora of Babylonian gods. It was the ultimate insult and God was not silent. Suddenly a hand appeared, its fingers scribing a message on the plaster wall: "MENE, MENE, TEKEL, PARSIN" (Daniel 5:25). The king paled and shook in fear. He called out his team of enchanters, astrologers and diviners, but no one could interpret the message. Finally Daniel was called. To him the message was obvious. Daniel gave Belshazzar a brief history lesson, reminding him of the humility his father learned through his lapse into insanity. Then Daniel summed it up:

But you his son, O Belshazzar, have not humbled yourself, though you knew all this.

Instead, you have set yourself up against the Lord of heaven. . . .

> This is what these words mean:
> *Mene*: God has numbered the days of your reign and brought it to an end.
> *Tekel*: You have been weighed on the scales and found wanting.
> *Peres* [singular of Parsin]: Your kingdom is divided and given to the Medes and Persians. (5:22, 26-28)

The shaken Belshazzar rewarded Daniel, making him the third highest ruler in Bablyon. It was an empty reward. That night Babylon fell in a joint Median and Persian invasion. Belshazzar died in the conflict.

We Reap What We Sow

I refer to these two biblical stories to emphasize a simple point: we reap what we sow. Sow in accordance to faith and you'll reap miracles. Sow in accordance to sin and you'll reap disaster. It is a principle so universal that we even see it in nature. If you want green beans, plant green beans. Carrot seeds will produce carrots. Flowers spring from flower seeds, and so on. Indeed, if it was otherwise, the whole predictability and morality of life would be at stake.

Yet it is just at this simple truth that Satan so often launches his greatest deception. As probably happened with Belshazzar, Satan skillfully deceives us into thinking that this principle of sowing and reaping will be temporarily suspended to surfeit our own lust. He whispers, "Go ahead. Do it just this once.

Who will know, and what difference will it make anyway?" Foolishly we are drawn astray only to realize later how deceived we were.

Such a principle is a strong deterrent. The sting of a bitter harvest is enough to make most of us learn and remember our lesson the next time we are tempted. But this principle contains a seed of encouragement as well. Galatians 6:7-8 says:

> Do not be deceived: God cannot be mocked. A man reaps what he sows. The one who sows to please his sinful nature, from that nature will reap destruction; the one who sows to please the Spirit, from the Spirit will reap eternal life.

We reap what we sow, but our harvest need not be bitter. We can sow seeds for a righteous harvest as easily as we can sow our "wild oats." How do we "sow to the Spirit?" We sow by simply responding to God in obedience and faith. Remember the boy that yielded his small meal to Jesus? The harvest that day was over 5,000 satisfied people. Or how about the prostitute that came boldly to Simon's house the day Jesus was there? Steeling herself against the Pharisees' ridicule, she opened a jar of perfume and anointed Jesus, washing His feet with her tears and wiping them with her hair. Jesus said, "I tell you the truth, wherever this gospel is preached throughout the world, what she has done will also be told, in memory of her" (Matthew 26:13). The despised prostitute had reaped a place in history through her generous seeds of worship.

By faith Ruth left her country as a penniless widow

and returned with her mother-in-law to Israel. God honored her faith, and provided for her needs. What's more, this unlikely woman also became part of Christ's ancestral line and the great-grandmother of King David (Matthew 1:5-16).

Rahab, the Gentile prostitute, was also spared certain death and given a place in Christ's lineage because in faith she hid and helped the Jewish spies (Joshua 2; 6:25; Matthew 1:5). Noah survived the flood (Genesis 7-8). Moses delivered Israel (Exodus 7-14). Peter healed the sick, and Paul cast out demons (Acts 9:32-43; 16:16-18). All of these miracles and many, many more were the harvest of decisions made and service rendered in faith. Obedience and faith—this is sowing to the Spirit.

Meager Sowing Means Meager Harvest

But not only do we reap what we sow, we also reap in accordance with the amount sown. Second Corinthians 9:6 says: "Whoever sows sparingly will also reap sparingly, and whoever sows generously will also reap generously."

Have you ever noticed that the harvest a farmer reaps is always more than the seed he has sown? Few people would be in farming if this wasn't so. It is a principle we've come to rely on, and the same applies to the spiritual realm. If we sow sparingly, we will reap sparingly. If we sow generously, the harvest will in turn be generous. But what exactly does sowing generously mean?

One day Jesus was in the temple watching people place their tithe in the treasury. Many wealthy people came by. Some no doubt gave seeking praise for their generosity. Others were just doing their part. Finally along came a poor widow. Her offering consisted of two small copper coins. Financially it was nearly worthless. But Jesus immediately pointed her out to the disciples. He said:

> I tell you the truth, this poor widow has put more into the treasury than all the others. They all gave out of their wealth; but she, out of her poverty, put in everything—all she had to live on. (Mark 12:43-44)

She gave "all she had." So did the little boy who offered up his meager lunch to Jesus the day so many were hungry. How do you approach your life or ministry with Jesus? Do you hold back and just give your due, or is your life fully His? When we lay our all on the altar before Him, we are sowing generously, and the harvest to come will be generous as well.

One weekend my husband and I drove to Portland, Oregon, to visit the seminary he hoped to attend. It all seemed perfect except for one thing—finances. We had decided to use our savings to pay for his schooling, but soon realized that would only cover half of a year's tuition. Scott had three and a half years of intensive study ahead. Financially there was simply no way. In faith, we decided to move. Scott would attend until the money ran out. I took a part-time job; Scott worked as manager of the apartment complex where we lived. Still our monthly income was far below expenses. But God worked. In the next three and a half years, Scott finished seminary without an interruption, we had our first child and Scott was even able to go on a missions trip to South America. When we left seminary, we not only walked away debt free, but with the original amount in our savings that we had come with!

This experience has been repeated time and again for us. Sometimes God's blessing has been affordable medical or dental care. Sometimes it's been a vacation beyond our wildest dreams, let alone finances! Once we needed $800 to finance a move to the Midwest. We brought our concern to the Lord in prayer. A few days later I went to the post office to get our mail. In our box was a check and letter that went something like this:

> We've heard of your decision to seek additional training in ministry by moving to the Midwest for a specialized year of internship. We'd like to help. Enclosed is a check for $815 to get you started.

I'm not ashamed to tell you that I stood in the post office that day and wept. God is so good when we give it all to Him.

It Takes Time

But what about when the blessings seem long in coming? Has God failed, or our giving been insufficient? A third harvest principle is patience. Although the harvest will come, there will be many days of sunshine and rain in between. James 5:7-8 says:

> Be patient, then, brothers, until the Lord's coming. See how the farmer waits for the land to yield its valuable crop and how patient he is for the autumn and spring rains. You too, be

patient and stand firm, because the Lord's coming is near.

Do you remember the first time you planted a garden? How you watched for those first sprouts to appear? Daily you watered, weeded and waited for that first harvest. At times you may have despaired, but harvest always came. All it took was faithfulness and patience.

Natural harvests may fail of course, but God protects our spiritual harvest. This is why Paul encourages, "Let us not become weary in doing good, for at the proper time we will reap a harvest if we do not give up" (Galatians 6:9). It is so easy to become discouraged and want to give up. But don't despair; God has promised you a harvest. It just takes time.

One Sunday afternoon there was a knock on the door at my parents' home. When my father opened the door, there stood a man he hadn't seen for 14 years! As Ken reintroduced himself, he asked permission to share what God had done in his life. The afternoon shadows lengthened as his amazing story unfolded.

Fourteen years ago, Ken and my father had worked together. During that time, my father had said some things to Ken regarding his need to trust Christ as Savior. But Ken wanted no part of Christ. Shortly after that, career changes led both men in separate directions.

Ken admittedly tried to push my dad's witness from his mind. But as Ken's marriage began to unravel, the Holy Spirit continued to speak to his heart. In the year following his divorce, Ken gave his heart to Christ. His family eventually became Christians, and Ken and his wife were remarried. "So I just wanted to stop by and thank you for what you said to me those many years ago," Ken concluded. "As you can see, my marriage has been saved and my entire family has come to Christ as a result!"

Jesus likened the kingdom of heaven to a crop sown in faith. After the farmer had done his part, there was nothing left but to wait for the harvest (Mark 4:26-29). Just so, seeds of righteousness sown today will ultimately result in a great harvest for the kingdom of heaven. We have God's word on it.

When We Share Another's Harvest

Does this mean that all the hardships of life are the harvest of personal disobedience? Certainly not! We live in a sin-warped world. Because of Adam and Eve's disobedience, all mankind has entered life spiritually separated from God which means hardship—physically and spiritually—for each of us. We are not personally accountable for such conditions; this is simply the natural state of mankind.

The repercussions of Adam and Eve's original sin are experienced both in the heartaches we bring on ourselves and those that come unbidden. Our bitter harvest may be hard to take at times. Yet bitter still is unjustly suffering under the unrighteous harvest of another. How are we to respond when life seems so unfair?

David experienced many injustices in his own life. For starters, he was pursued by the obsessed King Saul. Hardly the reward a faithful military leader should receive. And in his last years as king, David was mocked as he fled in exile from his own throne (2 Samuel 16).

But the story that best underlines dealing with injustice is told in First Samuel 25, and the teacher is an ordinary housewife. Abigail's husband, Nabal, was a selfish, evil, impudent man. His name means "fool" and even Abigail acknowledged that he did indeed live up to the reputation.

It seems David had formed a ragtag band of soldiers who rented themselves out as protection for various needs. Over the past months David's men had protected Nabal's sheep and shepherds from harm as they pastured their flocks. Now the season for shearing had come. This was typically a time of great celebration, so David sent messengers to Nabal to receive their reward for the protective services they had rendered. Instead of reward, Nabal scorned David's men.

> "Who is this David?" Nabal asked. "Who is this son of Jesse? Many servants are breaking away from their masters these days. Why should I take my bread and water, and the meat I have slaughtered for my shearers, and give it to men coming from who knows where?" (1 Samuel 25:10-11)

When David's men repeated Nabal's selfish, scornful message to David, he was furious! "Put on your swords!" David commanded (25:13). Then he led an angry march to take by force the reward unjustly denied them.

Meanwhile Abigail, informed by a servant of all

that had unfolded between Nabal and David, went to intercede. If David attacked, innocent lives would be lost on both sides. She took food to David and his men. When David saw her, he complained to her.

It's been useless—all my watching over this fellow's property in the desert so that nothing of his was missing. He has paid me back evil for good. May God deal with David, be it ever so severely, if by morning I leave alive one male of all who belong to him! (25:21-22)

She could understand his anger. Her husband had been unfair. But Abigail also understood that seeking revenge was not the answer. Humbling herself before him, Abigail began to teach David a lesson in forgiveness. "May my lord pay no attention to that wicked man Nabal," she said. "He is just like his name—his name is Fool, and folly goes with him" (25:25).

Seek to Be Understanding

The first step in forgiveness is understanding. Not the kind of understanding that knows all the motivations behind a person's reactions. Only God truly knows the heart of man. But the kind of understanding that recognizes and accepts a person for who he is. Abigail described her husband as a foolish man. This wasn't some caustic remark uttered behind his back, it was a plea for understanding. In effect she was saying, "This is just the way my husband is. It is no surprise that he has done something like this, for he is a foolish man."

Sarah taught me a similar lesson in forgiveness as

we sat near a playground watching our children play one lazy afternoon. Line by line she shared with me her upbringing in an emotionally abusive home. Neither her mother nor her father had reinforced her worth as a person. As she put it, "I spent most of my life feeling I had been some kind of cosmic mistake." Her hunger for love had led to promiscuous adolescent experiences. And while her immoral lifestyle ended after marriage, her mental addiction to lust raged on. Finally, Sarah sought the help of a counselor. By God's grace, deliverance became hers.

When I asked her how she felt about her parents, she responded: "At first I was angry. I mean, how could they do this to me—refuse their own child the love and acceptance I needed? But in time I understood that they had loved me the best they were able. They too had been victims of their past."

David Augsburger, in his book *The Freedom of Forgiveness 70 X 7*, wrote, "Understanding underlies forgiveness! . . . When we have learned to look about us with the loving eyes of Christ no man is unlovable, no man is beyond forgiving" (1970 27, 30). And isn't this how we would have others treat us? Don't we all long to have others look beyond our ugly reactions and treat us with understanding and acceptance? If we stand in need of such mercy (and we all do at times), we dare not begrudge it to others. If you want to resist revenge, start by being understanding to your enemy.

Decide to Forgive

The next step is to decide quickly to forgive. Consciously surrender your bitterness to Jesus

Christ. Abigail pleaded with David, "Please forgive your servant's offense" (25:28). (Apparently the identity of the wife was one with her husband in this culture. His successes, his failures, were considered her own. This would explain why Abigail assumed responsibility to ask David's forgiveness for an offense given by her husband.)

But why should he? David was cheated from his due. Every fiber of his being cried for justice, not pardon! Yet Abigail knew that bitterness and vengeance exact a high price. Revenge, no matter how wronged we have been, is never right. And nothing can harden the soul faster than bitterness. This is why the Bible counsels Christians to forgive and forbear with one another. Forgiveness, impossible as it may seem at times, is the path to life in its fullness.

Sarah also told me that deciding to forgive her parents was the toughest part of recovery. "For a long time I let anger and bitterness dictate my feelings toward them. I didn't want to rebuild our relationship. Instead I hoped to withdraw until communication between us quit completely. Then one day I remembered that God loves me unconditionally. It would be wrong not to extend them the same acceptance. No matter how justified my feelings were, I knew I had to forgive. Besides," Sarah said smiling, "I knew if I held onto my bitterness, I'd be the one to suffer."

How right Sarah is. David Augsburger wrote, "Revenge is the most worthless weapon in the world. It ruins the avenger while more firmly confirming the enemy in his wrong. It initiates an endless flight down the bottomless stairway of rancor, reprisals and ruthless retaliation" (1970, 13). The greatest sufferer of unforgiveness is the one who withholds it. Decide to forgive.

Entrust Yourself to God's Sovereignty

Is there justice then for those who suffer the wrongs of others? The answer is—yes. Justice exists in the character of God, and it is implemented most perfectly when left in His sovereign hands. Abigail reminded David of his need to trust God's sovereignty, by referring to the past injustices he had suffered from King Saul. He had lived years in hiding, pursued relentlessly, simply because of the obsessive jealously of King Saul. Yet David had survived. Abigail pointed out that David escaped King Saul not because of his own vengeance, but because of his reliance on God's sovereignty. As a result, David's life was "bound securely in the bundle of the living by the LORD" (25:29). I like that verse. It reminds me that life is found in Jesus Christ and nowhere else; even when we are suffering unjustly (Colossians 3:3).

Leave Revenge to God

Abigail also mentioned that David had been fighting the Lord's battles. Yet this battle (David's plans for revenge) was not God's way. I wonder, who am I fighting for in the rub of daily life? Am I choosing spiritual warfare, or am I busy trying to even the score on various personal grievances? Justice is assured if we leave our heartaches with the Lord. He sees our situation and will avenge where there is wrong (Romans 12:19).

Another reason to forgive is that the forgiving heart

walks away from conflict with a clean conscience. Abigail reminded David of this treasure. "When the LORD . . . has appointed [David] leader over Israel, my master will not have on his conscience the staggering burden of needless bloodshed or of having avenged himself" (1 Samuel 25:30-31).

And what a burden regret can be! Words spoken, and actions taken in the heat of anger can take a lifetime to undo. How often have you said, "If I only had it to do over? . . . " Revenge imparts a hollow and costly victory. It is always the better choice, to abstain and leave vengeance with God. He will turn your heartache into blessing, if you surrender your injustices to Him. Before we parted company that day, Sarah shared a testimony that challenged my own outlook on life's difficulties.

"You know," she said seriously as her blue eyes met mine. "I used to resent my past—the scars, heartache and continuing struggles that seemed so unfair. But recently, I've come to thank God for my difficulties. I can see now that my weaknesses keep me close to God. Without Him, I'd be unable to remain faithful to my husband and parent my children as God would have me. So, in a sense, the unfair emotional abuse I suffered as a child has resulted in a deepening dependence on God, and a richer appreciation for His grace. I don't know that my walk with God would be so close without the struggles I've had."

Romans 8:28 says, "And we know that in all things God works for the good of those who love him." And, amazing as it may seem, "all things" certainly includes injustices. For the Christian, every rain cloud of injustice does indeed have a silver lining of blessing.

Focusing on Christ

How can you forgive? How can you stop sowing seeds of unrighteousness and begin sowing for a harvest of eternal reward? By focusing on Christ. The successful Christian experience is a life lived united to Christ. As we learn to draw our life from Him, we find the strength to resist revenge. What others do to us begins to matter far less than the spiritual realities that no one can touch. He is our life, not the circumstances surrounding us.

By focusing on Christ, we find the strength to be faithful in service, even when our harvest seems long in coming. Through Christ we also find the discernment to know how and where to invest our energies for God's kingdom. He's both the foundation and the overseer of every harvest. It all centers on Him.

Still, sometimes living God's way seems incredibly hard. He calls us to forsake our natural response for self-protection and promotion, while others that live in contradiction to God's Word seem often to reap the blessings that pass God's faithful by. In our hearts we wonder if the Christian life is really worth it. And what about rewards? Does the Christian life really pay? This is the subject we want to look at next.

MAKING IT YOURS

1. What is the biblical principle of investment mentioned in Galatians 6:7-8?

2. What two types of spiritual investment must a person choose between in life? (Galatians 6:8)

3. How does a person "sow to please the Spirit?" (Galatians 5:16, 24-25)

4. Read 2 Corinthians 9:6. What is the biblical principle of investment given here?

5. Does sowing generously mean simply giving a lot financially to God's work? According to these passages, how would you define a generous sower? (Mark 12:41-44; John 6:1-13)

6. The fact that sometimes the return on spiritual investments seems long in coming underlines another principle of investment. Read Galatians 6:9. What investment principle is given in this verse?

7. No one operates alone in life's investment process. The consequences we reap also affect all those around us. It seems unfair (and indeed often is) when we end up sharing a bitter harvest that another has sowed. According to 1 Samuel 25:2-38, what injustice did David and his men suffer because of Nabal's selfishness?

8. David's immediate response was to seek revenge, but Abigail interceded. What four-part lesson did she teach David about forgiveness?
   • 1 Samuel 25:25
   • 1 Samuel 25:26-28a
   • 1 Samuel 25:28b-29
   • 1 Samuel 25:30-31

9. Revenge is a natural instinct to pain. Yet the Bible gives three good reasons why we should leave revenge with God. What are they?

- Romans 12:19
- Genesis 50:20
- 1 Samuel 25:31

Chapter Ten

Does Christian Living Really Pay?

WHEN I WAS IN COLLEGE, there was a professor who had the gracious practice of excusing any graduating senior from his final exam. Needless to say, he was well-known on campus for this policy. Wisely I scheduled this required course for the final semester of my senior year. But the first day of class I received a terrible shock.

"It has always been my practice in the past," the professor said, "to excuse graduating seniors from the final exam. However, I've reconsidered that policy and decided that the seniors should take the final along with everyone else."

I couldn't believe my ears! "How could he do this to me?" I fumed angrily. I'd done my time at the books. I was due this break! I was furious!

As I look back at this event now, I have to laugh at myself. Was my teacher unfair? Of course not. But

143

he had been generous to other students in the past, and jealousy had seized my heart. In fact, my reaction was every bit like those in two parables that Jesus used.

The disciples had left everything (homes, families, incomes, prestige) to wander with Jesus. I doubt any of us has been called to the complete dedication that these men were. It was a hard life. One day Peter asked Jesus if it was really worth it to follow Him. "We have left everything to follow you!" Peter said. "What then will there be for us?" (Matthew 19:27).

Jesus answered Peter with a promise. He said:

> I tell you the truth . . . when the son of Man sits on his glorious throne, you who have followed me will also sit on twelve thrones, judging the twelve tribes of Israel. And everyone who has left houses or brothers or sisters or father or mother or children or fields for my sake will receive a hundred times as much and will inherit eternal life. But many who are first will be last, and many who are last will be first. (19:28-30)

The Laborers in the Vineyard Parable

Then Jesus told a parable. He told the story of a landowner that went out to hire laborers to work in his vineyard. He hired some workers in the morning and contracted to pay them a denarius (a usual day's wage) for their work. Later, around nine in the morning, he hired additional workers, also promising them a denarius at the day's end. Still more workers were hired at noon, three o'clock and five o'clock, all with the same promised wages (*The New*

Testament and Wycliffe Bible Commentary 1971, 70).
When the day came to an end, the landowner paid
his workers. Each received a denarius as promised.
Those hired at five o'clock were delighted. Imagine,
a whole day's wage for only an hour's work! But
those hired before nine were angry! " 'These men
who were hired last worked only one hour,' they said,
'and you have made them equal to us who have
borne the burden of the work and the heat of the
day' " (20:12).

The landowner listened but held his ground. "He
answered one of them, 'Friend, I am not being
unfair to you. Didn't you agree to work for a
denarius? Take your pay and go. I want to give the
man who was hired last the same as I gave you.
Don't I have the right to do what I want with my
own money? Or are you envious because I am
generous?' " (20:13-15).

Then Jesus repeated the statement that preceded
the parable. He said, "So the last will be first, and
the first will be last" (20:16).

But doesn't this story contradict what Jesus told
Peter in chapter 19? It seems Jesus promised Peter
that sacrifice in the Christian life would be
rewarded. Then He told the parable of the vineyard
workers where those that sacrificed little ended up
with the better deal.

We Serve a Generous God

Clearly this story refers to our service for God. It
has no reference to salvation, for our salvation is
already the gift of a generous God. We can, in fact,
do nothing to earn it (Ephesians 2:8-9). Yet even in
service, it is God's generosity that is highlighted. In

this story the landowner generously paid the workers hired last the same as those hired first. It may seem improper to us, but seen through God's heart of generous love, such a reward is totally fitting.

The parable also underlines the fact that we can never out give God. Whether our service is meager or great, we will indeed receive at least what is fair. What was it that Jesus promised to Peter? Everyone who sacrifices for God's kingdom will "receive a hundred times as much and will inherit eternal life" (Matthew 19:29). Clearly, God is no man's debtor.

But what about that puzzling reminder that "Many who are first will be last, and many who are last will be first" (19:30)? Jesus is referring to a difference in perspectives. Only God knows the heart of man and can reward perfectly. It may be that what we see as first place in terms of sacrifice is in fact last place before God.

The Prodigal Son

Jesus highlighted this issue of service in another well-known parable of the Prodigal Son in Luke 15. The story goes that a man had two sons. One son was comfortable with pursuing his livelihood working alongside his father, but the younger boy longed to make his own way in the world. One day the need to part ways became obvious. At the boy's urging, the father gave his younger son his inheritance and the boy soon packed and left. He finally settled in some far off country. There he foolishly squandered his inheritance in a spree of wild living until he was penniless and destitute. What's worse a famine hit this country at the same time, so there was simply no charity to be found. To survive, he took work as a swineherd. Even so, he was still so hungry he longed to eat the mash fed the pigs.

So life continued until one day it occurred to him that he might possibly go back home. "Maybe if I humble myself before my father and beg his forgiveness, he'll at least take me in as a servant," he thought to himself. "I'm no longer worthy to be regarded as his son, but even the hired hands eat better than I do now." And thus he began the journey home.

On the other end, the father had never given up hope that his headstrong son would one day return. Often the father's gaze wandered to the path leading to his door, hoping to see his son's familiar form. Just as often, his hopes were unfulfilled. Then one day he saw someone coming. Was it his son? He was a long way off. It was hard to tell. But then he was sure. Yes—it was his son—and in an instant he was running with all his might to meet him. As he drew closer, he could see the boy's gaunt, ragged form. If it had been anyone else, he might have been put off, but the father didn't hesitate. Instead he threw his arms around his son in a mighty embrace. How long had it been since he'd left? He couldn't remember, but it didn't matter now. The son, lost for so long, had finally come home. The father's heart was wild with joy!

The boy tried to deliver his apology. No doubt he'd been over it a hundred times on the long journey home, but his father wouldn't hear it. The past was over and forgiven. Now it was time for rejoicing.

"Quick!" said the father. "Bring the best robe and

put it on him. Put a ring on his finger and sandals on his feet. Bring the fattened calf and kill it. Let's have a feast and celebrate. For this son of mine was dead and is alive again; he was lost and is found" (Luke 15:22-24).

It was a great party. But not everyone was happy. As the celebration got underway, the older son came in from the field. It was obvious something was afoot. When he inquired of one of the servants, the story of his baby brother's return spilled out. Standing there watching the celebration, the elder brother's heart turned to stone. Angry jealousy consumed him and he refused to join the celebration. Finally his father came out to talk with him.

"Look!" the son shouted angrily. "All these years I've been slaving for you and never disobeyed your orders. Yet you never gave me even a young goat so I could celebrate with my friends. But when this son of yours who has squandered your property with prostitutes comes home, you kill the fattened calf for him" (15:29-30).

I must commend the father on his answer. I would probably have delivered an attitude lecture. Instead this wise dad looked his son in the eyes and said, "My son, . . . you are always with me, and everything I have is yours. But we had to celebrate and be glad, because this brother of yours was dead and is alive again; he was lost and is found" (15:31-32).

Did you get the point? Like the father in this parable, like the generous landowner, we, too, serve a generous God. Because of Jesus Christ, we've been made co-inheritors with the Son of God! All the riches of God are ours. And what did any of us

do to deserve such a reward? Nothing. Absolutely
nothing. To serve such a God is a privilege. If we are
jealously comparing our blessings with our brothers
and sisters, then our eyes are focused in the wrong
direction.

Defining Rewards

Still God in His generosity goes one step farther.
He not only gives us the privilege of serving Him,
but promises to reward us as well. Yet if these
rewards exclude salvation, just what are they? Are
they the same as temporal blessings or different?

The dictionary defines a reward as "something
that is given in return for good or evil done . . .
especially that is offered or given for some service"
(*Webster's New Collegiate Dictionary* 1974, 993). A
reward differs from a blessing in that it is merited.
Blessings may or may not be merited. This is why
Jesus mentioned that God "causes his sun to rise on
the evil and the good, and sends rain on the
righteous and the unrighteous" (Matthew 5:45). We
are all constant recipients of God's blessings, but we
merit few of them. And while blessings in the Bible
are usually referred to in a temporal context,
rewards are generally spoken of as being received or
experienced later in eternity.

The Bible mentions a number of rewards specifically. In James 1:12 and Revelation 2:10 we read of
one—the crown of life. James says, "Blessed is the
man who perseveres under trial, because when he
has stood the test, he will receive the crown of life
that God has promised to those who love him."
Revelation 2:10 refers to this crown as that which is
awarded to those who suffer persecution and mar-

tyrdom. "Be faithful, even to the point of death, and I will give you the crown of life."

In First Corinthians 9:24-27 Paul likens the Christian experience to competing in a marathon. He says that many run, but only the disciplined runner gets the prize. Of course, those who run earthly marathons win earthly, temporal trophies. Paul's aim was to live such a disciplined life that he would one day win "a crown that will last forever."

Then in First Thessalonians 2:19 Paul mentions another kind of crown—that which consists of the lives we've brought to Christ. Some translations refer to this as our "crown of exultation" (NASB). It may be that a verse in Daniel can illuminate our understanding of this crown a bit further. It reads: "Those who are wise will shine like the brightness of the heavens, and those who lead many to righteousness, like the stars for ever and ever" (12:3).

What an awesome thought that soul-winners will someday be as radiant as the stars! No wonder Paul referred to his converts as "our hope, our joy, or the crown in which we will glory in the presence of our Lord Jesus" (1 Thessalonians 2:19).

And there are still other rewards. Second Timothy 4:8 refers to the "crown of righteousness" which Paul eagerly anticipated as he awaited his martyrdom in Rome. This is God's reward for faithful service and a heart that longs for Christ's return. And it wasn't just for Paul. He wrote:

> Now there is in store for me the crown of righteousness, which the Lord, the righteous Judge, will award to me on that day—and not

only to me, but also to all who have longed for his appearing. (2 Timothy 4:8)

First Peter 5:4 promises the crown of unfading glory to those who are faithful and obedient to God in pastoral ministry. And Jesus promises an equally impressive reward to those who assist pastors. He said:

> Anyone who receives a prophet because he is a prophet will receive a prophet's reward, and anyone who receives a righteous man because he is a righteous man will receive a righteous man's reward. (Matthew 10:41)

In fact, God even keeps track of glasses of ice water when they are dispensed in love and support of His kingdom (10:42)! So perhaps it wouldn't hurt to fill up those trays and keep a few extra cubes handy. The point is, whether the sacrifice is little or large, God sees your faithfulness and will one day reward you.

This, of course, is not an exhaustive list of the rewards God has in store for Christians. The Bible presents these references as mere glimpses of God's goodness and faithfulness. No doubt God has countless other rewards in heaven, tailor-made for each of us.

The Purposes of Rewards

Yet when we consider all that Christ has given us, is it really necessary for God to bribe us with rewards? Isn't it rather shallow to set our sights on earning a crown? What is the point of a relationship with Christ, if it boils down to a collection of merit badges?

It is true that rewards are motivators. What parent doesn't know the power of a promised goody to a reluctant child? Our Heavenly Father knows this as well. We are self-centered by nature. We will never be free from it until we step into Christ's redeeming presence. True, it is rather crass that God must motivate us with rewards, but it is also realistic. This is why Paul admonishes the Corinthian Christians to get serious about investing their lives in eternal values. He wrote that each believer is given a foundation for life in Jesus Christ. What he builds on that foundation is up to him. If he builds by investing his life in the things that will last for eternity (i.e. his relationship with God and the influence he is for God in the world), then he will be rewarded. But if he invests his life in temporal pursuits (no matter how prestigious), these investments will be burned up when put to the test (1 Corinthians 3:10-15). Such a believer will still retain his salvation, but nothing more. Pursuing rewards may seem an infantile source of motivation. But remember, there is certainly no merit in refusing to pursue eternal rewards only to stand with a pile of temporal cinders at your feet.

But rewards are intended for another reason as well—to encourage us. Let's face it; life is downright tough. In our hearts, I think we've all wondered if the Christian life is really worth the sacrifices at times. When Paul was imprisoned in Rome, await-ing his execution, he took comfort in four things: that his life was almost over, the satisfaction in having done his best for Christ, that he would soon be in his Lord's presence and that his faithfulness would be rewarded (2 Timothy 4:7-8).

A promise has the power to inspire the faith to confront insurmountable odds. How else can we understand the human dramas of individuals who overcome handicaps or transform their characters to become incredible success stories. And these are often the result of mere human, fallible promises. The promises of God are even more inspiring. Thus Hebrews 11 summarizes the great feats of faith as inspired by one thing—the promise of God. If all these great saints of the past needed the promised rewards of God to help them remain faithful, we stand in good company should we need to claim them ourselves on dark days.

Rewards also reflect the character of God. They are reminders of His faithfulness, love and generosity. Could serving such a King ever be a disappointment? He may not meet our expectation at the moment, but never are we short-changed with Christ.

Last, rewards are given to someday deepen our experience of worship. First Corinthians 13 contains God's definition of love. But before Paul describes love, he has an interesting statement about service. He says:

> If I speak in the tongues of men and of angels, but have not love, I am only a resounding gong or a clanging cymbal. If I have the gift of prophecy and can fathom all mysteries and all knowledge, and if I have a faith that can move mountains, but have not love, I am nothing. If

I give all I possess to the poor and surrender my body to the flames, but have not love, I gain nothing. (13:1-3)

How much reward will the Christian earn who does not operate from a heart of love? Nothing. Even martyrdom is fruitless if the source of the deed is not love.

Love of God is the wellspring for true Christian service (Mark 12:30-31). God will reward us, but something happens along life's way. As we walk with Christ and grow to love and worship Him, we lose sight of the reward and see only the Rewarder. He is truly our reward.

I can think of no greater trophy than an Olympic gold medal. That symbol stands for dedication and excellence above and beyond the rest. If I owned such a medal, I'd have it framed and hanging on a wall for all my friends to see. And if I decided to give that to someone, I'd hand it over with pride and tenderness. The last thing I would do would be to throw it at his or her feet! Yet a throne room glimpse in Revelation 4 reveals the 24 elders doing just that with the crowns they had been given. But you see, when we stand before Jesus, our trophies will pale by comparison in His radiant presence. They will be all we have to offer—our best —yet not even worthy to pass from our hands to His!

A Genuine Relationship

Does Christian living really pay? Yes it does, but only if our experience springs from a genuine relationship with Jesus Christ. A spiritual charade, no matter how convincing, will always be a hollow experience.

I was raised in a strong Christian home, where my parents faithfully modeled Christianity for my brothers and me. Some of my earliest memories revolve around the many activities we attended at church. Among those memories is a week at summer camp where I invited Christ to come into my life. I can't say that I understood my decision very well, only that I wanted to avoid hell. According to my counselor, praying to receive Christ was the way one escaped such a destiny. Surrender of the control of my life was never covered or was beyond my childish understanding.

Still, I desired to be a good Christian, and over the years developed a mental picture of what that would be. My definition mainly was a legalistic set of dos and don'ts; a definition I set out to religiously observe.

I lived by this creed until I went to an out-of-state, Christian liberal arts college that supposedly admitted only Christians. What I saw on campus shocked me. All around me, students were pursuing lifestyles that were far from Christian. I was confused. They seemed to be having such fun, while my superficial faith rang hollow. Doubt began to eat away at my values. Had I been duped? Could it be that the Christian life really wasn't worth the sacrifice after all?

About this time I was taking a psychology class that left me questioning whether the Bible was indeed the absolute basis for moral truth. Although he was supposedly a Christian man (and hard at work on his doctorate in Christian education), my professor's lectures left me confused as to which he valued more, the Bible or the theories of psychology. So I made an appointment to talk with him.

Sitting in his office that day I explained my confusion. "There has to be some bottom line," I said to him. "Most of these psychologists are atheists or agnostics. Not everyone can be right. What do you think is the absolute basis of truth?"

The professor looked across the desk and into my eyes. "I don't know," he said. "And if you ever find out, please come and tell me."

I was devastated. I'd expected him to say truth is found in Jesus Christ, or that he based his life on the Word of God. But not this—I'd never expected this! As I walked out of his office, I was seething with anger and despair. *Well,* I thought to myself, *if he doesn't know and he's working on his doctorate, how will I ever know? There really must not be a God. And if there is a God, He certainly doesn't care about me. What's more, I don't care about Him either!*

From that point on I lived only for the moment. For me, there was no right or wrong—no rules to live by. Common sense kept me out of any serious wrongdoing, but in my heart I had totally forsaken my Christian upbringing.

I expected to be happy. And for a time I reveled in my rebel freedom. But before long I found I was still hungering for meaning and purpose in life. I soon discovered I wanted something greater than the pursuit of my own selfish passions.

Fortunately, Jeannine played on a softball team with me. I knew Jeannine from some classes we shared and teased her mercilessly for the integrity she took in her work. She must have sensed my spiritual need, but she never said anything. Instead, her life spoke the message I couldn't ignore. For Jeannine had a peace about her that I hungered for and couldn't understand. Finally one night I could contain my curiosity no longer. Stopping by her room, I said, "Jeannine, this relationship with Jesus Christ—it really means something to you, doesn't it?"

I'll never forget her answer. "Cheryl," she said, "it's everything!"

A short time later I somehow came across this verse in Philippians 1:6: "Being confident of this, that he who began a good work in you will carry it on to completion until the day of Christ Jesus." I realized for the first time that I couldn't change myself and that God had never expected me to. No wonder my legalistic approach to Christianity hadn't worked. I had never surrendered! I realized now that He would do everything if I would only give Him the chance. That night, in tears and great shouts of joy, I surrendered my life to Christ. It was truly a turning point, for my walk with Him has never been the same. It is deeper, richer, fuller than anything I imagined possible. Now I can echo, as my friend testified to me—life with Christ is everything!

It hasn't always been easy. My husband and I have experienced many of the normal heartaches of life and ministry. And there have been times when I've been tempted again to give up and walk away. Has life with Christ been worth it, you ask? Yes, but not because I'm earning a reward in heaven. Life with

Christ became worthwhile when I quit pretending to be a Christian and fell in love with my Savior.

What is your testimony? Is Jesus Lord of your life, or just the name on your creed? Do you have a faith that springs from a well of love and devotion to Him? Do you have a faith that will carry you through the week—the year—through the difficulties as well as the blessings? Rewards will someday be handed out to God's faithful. But the answer to whether the Christian life is really worthwhile lies in your heart. Peter wrote, "Though you have not seen [Christ], you love him; . . . and are filled with an inexpressible and glorious joy" (1 Peter 1:8). Love is the key. How about it, does your Christian life really pay?

MAKING IT YOURS

1. After comparing the parable of the Prodigal Son in Luke 15:11-32 and the parable of the Laborers in the Vineyard in Matthew 20:1-16, what do you think Jesus was teaching about rewards through these parables?

2. What do you think Jesus meant when he said, "Many who are first will be last, and many who are last will be first"? (Matthew 19:30; 20:16)

3. How would you define "reward"?

4. Are blessings and rewards the same thing? Explain.

5. The rewards described in Scripture are intended as mere glimpses of God's goodness and faithfulness. How would you describe the rewards promised in the passages listed below?

- Matthew 10:41-42
- 1 Corinthians 9:24-27
- 2 Timothy 4:6-8
- 1 Peter 5:2-4
- Revelation 2:10; James 1:12

6. What are some reasons God promises us rewards?

7. What should motivate us to serve God above all else? (Mark 12:30-31; 1 Corinthians 13:3)

Chapter Eleven

Success Begins on Your Knees

I WAS EMOTIONALLY NUMB as the nurse handed me our newborn baby girl. Twenty-nine hours of labor and a brutal forceps delivery had taken all I had. I was grateful Sierra was healthy, but I was also grateful it was over. The experience had been a nightmare, far from the wonderful birthing experiences I had viewed on film in my Lamaze classes.

And recovery wasn't easy either. Because I had hemorrhaged during delivery, I had become very anemic. It would be months before my strength returned. In the meantime, I crawled through the day/night blur that life with a newborn creates. Sierra was a colicky baby. And while I longed for sleep, relaxing into blissful slumber seemed the farthest thing from her mind. To make matters worse, my husband was finishing his final and toughest semester in seminary. While he was away in the peace and quiet of the library, I was at home walking the floors with a fussy baby! It was certainly not the mothering experience I had anticipated. I was tired, bored and lonely. And to tell the truth, I'm not sure who cried more those first months—Sierra or me.

Time passed, however, and Sierra and I both grew up a little. She agreed to sleep through the night. I agreed to expand my self-centered ways to accommodate her needs. Scott graduated, and we accepted a pastorate in western Washington. On the whole, life seemed to be improving. But God had a surprise for us.

"I don't know if this is good news or not," my doctor said, "but you're going to have another baby." A baby? At first I was overjoyed! Sierra was two now, and Scott and I had been talking about having another child. Now Michael was on the way! Yet another emotion wrestled with my joy—fear. My delivery with Sierra had been so hard, would it be that way again?

As the months passed, my fears grew. "Oh God," I prayed, "please don't let this delivery be like the last one. I'm so afraid. I could never go through that again! Please, God, please don't let it happen that way again." But my prayers seemed to bounce off the ceiling. Instead of finding peace, my anxiety continued to grow.

Then one day I came across a book of promises from the Bible. The passages were categorized according to need. I found the section on fear and looked it up.

So do not fear, for I am with you;

do not be dismayed, for I am your God.
I will strengthen you and help you;
I will uphold you with my righteous right
    hand. (Isaiah 41:10)

The words were like a lifeline thrown to a drowning man, and I clung to them. "Oh, God," I prayed again. "I'm so afraid of delivering this baby. But Your Word says I don't need to be afraid. It says that You are with me and promise to take care of me no matter what. Thank You, Lord for Your promise." I was still afraid, of course. Yet daily as I continued reading and praying about the promises of God, a change slowly took place. When the day came for Michael to arrive, I found I was totally at peace; confident that no matter what happened, God would take care of me.

The delivery was perfect this time, and when the doctor handed me our infant son, I wept. Unlike the tears I'd shed in fear, these were tears of joy for the new little boy God had given us, and tears of gratitude for a God who had indeed seen me through.

When I saw my doctor at a checkup some weeks following, he remarked on the delivery. "I couldn't believe the delivery," he said. "You had been so afraid. I was prepared for the worst. But it couldn't have gone better. What happened?" Looking up at him, I smiled and explained, "Success begins on your knees!"

The Importance of Worship

What do I mean, "success begins on your knees"? Simply that victory begins when we start worshiping the Victor—Jesus Christ. Once Christ spent 40 days fasting in the desert (Matthew 4:1-11). At the end of this time Satan came and tempted Him three times. Initially, Satan tempted Jesus to satisfy his gnawing hunger by turning stones into bread. When that failed, Satan twisted Scripture to frame a presumptuous second testing. But Jesus knew the difference between faith and presumption and Satan's ploy again failed. Finally, Christ was promised all the kingdoms of the world if He would just bow down and worship Satan. It must have been an awesome moment. One act of homage and Jesus would gain world dominion, escaping all the shame and agony of Calvary. But this was a temptation Jesus would not tolerate. "Away from me, Satan!" Jesus shouted. "For it is written: 'Worship the Lord your God, and serve him only' " (4:10). Nothing is more important in life than worship—not even self-preservation. Clearly, worship is the greatest of all God's commandments (22:37-38) and should enjoy first priority in our walk with Him.

What Is Worship?

But what is worship? Is it more than going to church? Is worship more than rituals?

Around 428 B.C. a worship service was held in Jerusalem. Because the Jews had been living in exile, it was the first such service that had been held in over 70 years (Tenney, [1975] 1976, 4:406-407). People came from everywhere to the capital Nehemiah and his workers had labored so hard to restore. As they gathered before one of the city's gates, Ezra (a priest) began to speak. It was a simple service. Beginning at daybreak, Ezra read and explained the law to the people until noon. (And you thought your pastor was long-winded!) When he finally finished, the people began responding. "Amen! Amen!" they shouted enthusiastically. Some knelt with their faces to the ground as an act of worship. Nearly everyone wept. In fact, so great was their reaction to God's Word that Nehemiah had to step forward and encourage them. "Go," he said, "enjoy choice food and sweet drinks, and send some to those who have nothing prepared. This day is sacred to our Lord. Do not grieve, for the joy of the Lord is your strength" (Nehemiah 8:10).

What followed was the greatest celebration of the Feast of Booths since the days of Joshua. People ate together and sent food to one another. No one could remember a time of worship to equal this. In all it had been a remarkable three-faceted experience in worship. They had listened to God's Word. They had responded in prayer/praise. And they had enjoyed an enriched time of fellowship together.

Approximately 500 years later another worship service would be held in Jerusalem. This time the laity would not be returning exiles, but Christians. Yet the two worship experiences bear a striking similarity. Consider the description of worship given us in Acts 2:42, 46-67:

> They devoted themselves to the apostles' teaching and to the fellowship, to the breaking of bread and to prayer. . . . Every day they continued to meet together in the temple courts. They broke bread in their homes and ate together with glad and sincere hearts, praising

God and enjoying the favor of all the people.

Three elements of worship stand out repeatedly between these two worship experiences: God's Word, a response to God's Word (prayer/praise) and fellowship. Applied personally, these elements of worship translate into three mandates: the need to expose ourselves to God's Word and Christian teaching/testimonies; the need to respond to God's Word in prayer or praise; and the need to allow our worship to affect the world around us.

Worship could actually be depicted as a triangle.

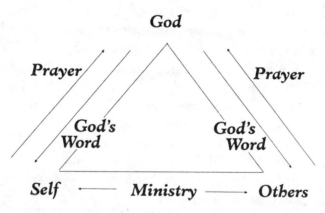

God is at the apex of the triangle. Others in addition to ourselves hold positions at the base of the triangle. God reveals Himself to us and others through His Word. We respond to God in prayer and service. In like manner, we also receive godly teaching through the ministry of others, and we may respond to others in prayer and ministry as well. As the entire triangle interrelates, the result is enriched fellow-ship. You see, true worship may begin in privacy between you and God, but it never ends there. True worship always touches those around us. In that sense, worship is never a solo experience.

God's Word—More Than a Vitamin

But to worship well, you must first lay a founda-tion for worship in God's Word. After all, it is the Bible that describes God to us, our relationship to Him and our place in the world. And Isaiah 55:11 promises that God's Word never goes out without accomplishing His purposes. Now that's power!

Yet too often many of us look at reading God's Word like taking vitamins. *It may help. It can't hurt. If I find the time, I'll squeeze it in.* How wrong we are to take such an attitude. I may not be sure of the merit of vitamins, but this much I do know, God's Word is far more than that. It is the foundation and power source of worship.

Praise Precedes Deliverance

Still another amazing characteristic is that God's Word always provokes a response. Usually this response is verbalized in prayer, and prayers of faith result in miracles. Recall for a moment my fear of delivering my second child. I tried almost everything to find peace. I listened to relaxation tapes, but they didn't help. The reassurance of friends was comfort-ing, but I was still afraid. I tried prayer; in a weak moment I even tried hypnosis. I tried everything I could think of and nothing seemed to work. But when I came to God's Word, began claiming His promises in faith, my mountain of fear began to crumble. The difference was faith-filled prayer, or what the Bible calls a "sacrifice of praise" (Hebrews 13:15).

It was a sacrifice of praise that made the difference when King Jehoshaphat found himself facing a mighty army. Moab, Ammon and Mount Seir had formed an alliance against the nation of Judah. When word reached King Jehoshaphat that his enemies were on the march toward Jerusalem, he proclaimed a national fast. The people responded. All across Judah the people came to Jerusalem to seek help from God. When they arrived, they amassed outside the temple, waiting for their king to speak. But rather than give the "State of the Union" address you and I might expect in such a situation, King Jehoshaphat prayed (2 Chronicles 20:6-12). True, the situation looked bleak. They must have all feared for the worst. But King Jehoshaphat made it clear where his focus was—his eyes were focused on Almighty God.

The next day they went out to battle. I'm sure many wondered what strategy the king had in mind. Never could they have anticipated what they heard. "Listen to me, Judah and people of Jerusalem!" said the king. "Have faith in the LORD your God and you will be upheld; have faith in his prophets and you will be successful" (20:20). Then he appointed a team of singers and praisers to lead them into battle. Can you imagine such a battle strategy? It would have been one day I especially wouldn't have wanted to be in the front lines. After all, the other side would be marching forward with weapons—not songs!

Yet as worship made the front line, and as they

went marching and singing to meet the enemy, God did an amazing thing. All at once the armies of Moab, Ammon, and Mount Seir turned and began fighting one another. Judah stood by and watched. When the battle ended, not a single survivor was left. The people of Judah went down on the battlefield and joyfully began to reap the spoils of war. It would take them three days to collect everything. So great was Judah's rejoicing that the battlefield was renamed the Valley of Beracah, meaning the Valley of Praise. Once again faith-filled prayer had made the difference.

Where is your focus when life gets tough? Are your prayers God-focused or self-focused? Hebrews 10:22 urges us to come to the throne of God, but it also urges that we "draw near to God with a sincere heart in full assurance of faith." Faith-filled prayer is the key to miracles. Not faith in what we want, but placing our faith in the promises and character of God.

Miracle in St. Croix

God once gave me the opportunity to travel to St. Croix to help with an Evangelism Explosion clinic being held there. (An Evangelism Explosion Clinic trains Christians to more effectively share their faith.) My part was to take teams of clinicians out witnessing every afternoon. Others had come to help as well. A gal named Teresa was among the volunteers. One day as we prepared to go out witnessing, Teresa came up to me.

"I don't know what to do," she confided. "I'm supposed to leave in a few minutes to take my team out witnessing and I feel miserable!" She looked pale and was feverish to the touch.

"Let me pray for you," I said. "God hasn't brought you all this way to get sick now."

Placing my hand on Teresa's shoulder we bowed our heads. "Oh, God," I prayed, "I thank You for the privilege you've given us to share Your gospel. And I know You haven't brought Teresa all this way only to have her get sick now. Satan would love to defeat us, but God, I pray asking You to bind Satan and bring healing to Teresa's body. Thank You, God, for hearing us. We look forward to seeing what You will do this afternoon as we go out."

We left then, and when we met some hours later, Teresa's face was aglow with excitement. "You won't believe what happened!" she exclaimed. "Remember how ill I was? Well, as the afternoon wore on, I felt better and better. Now I don't feel ill at all! What's more, my team was able to pray with a family of seven to receive Christ."

The Mystery of Prayer

Prayer is such a mystery—how God moves to touch a life with healing, save a marriage, change a circumstance. To know why God moves as He chooses is beyond my comprehension. As the Bible says:

> For [God's] thoughts are not your thoughts,
>   neither are your ways [God's] ways
> As the heavens are higher than the earth,
>   so are my ways higher than your ways
>   and my thoughts than your thoughts.
>   (Isaiah 55:8-9)

It would be wrong for me to promise a formula for

getting what you want from God in prayer. God is far greater than my grocery list of prayer requests. I remember once, as a child, explaining one of God's promises to my brother. "You know," I said earnestly, "the Bible says if two or more agree to ask God for something, God will do it (Matthew 18:19). So let's ask God for a swimming pool!" My brother agreed; it sounded like a great idea. So we folded our hands, squeezed our eyes shut, and sat there in the hot summer sunshine sending our faith-filled request heavenward. And as soon as I uttered "Amen," my brother and I were on our feet, running to the backyard to see if our pool had arrived. Of course, it hadn't. Back we went to pray another time or two. The results were always the same—no pool. Finally I decided I must have my "prayer formula" down wrong and we went off to play with the neighbor kids.

Funny, isn't it, the things we try as children? But we really don't grow to be all that much more sophisticated as adults. We still storm the gates of heaven with our faith-filled prayers. Some seem to be clearly based on God's promises and His revealed will, while we are unsure about others. The truth we all learn in time is that the answering part of prayer lies in His wise and loving hands. God chooses the answers and timing we need. Prayer/praise is but an opportunity to be part of that process, to be part of the victory He's planned. Nothing pleases God like faith. He delights to answer the heart that is raised in childlike trust.

I'd always laughed over my "pool prayer," until I was telling it to a friend this past year. "You know," she said, "even though God never filled your backyard with a pool, He did provide your family with a lake cabin soon thereafter. So God really did answer your prayer after all." I was astounded. The connection between my summers at the lake and my childhood prayer had never occurred to me before, and I stood happily rebuked. God really does answer when we pray in faith.

Worship Is Relational, Too

Worship doesn't end with the worshiper and God. True worship always affects those around us. The service in Ezra's day resulted in a festival of fellowship and praise never before experienced in Judah's national history. The New Testament Christians ate together regularly "enjoying the favor of all the people" (Acts 2:47). And while Judah rejoiced in their deliverance from Moab, Ammon and Mount Seir, the same testimony struck a fearful awe in the other nations surrounding them (2 Chronicles 20:29). As a result of my own worship experience, Teresa and her team led seven to saving faith in Christ; and my doctor wanted to know what made the difference in an easy delivery that he had expected to be so difficult. True worship will not only bring miracles, but will touch our world as well.

What overwhelming circumstances are you facing? Perhaps it is a ministry that doesn't seem to want to grow. Perhaps it is financial needs, or fears that seem unconquerable. Jesus promised, "If you have faith as small as a mustard seed, you can say to this mountain, 'Move from here to there' and it will move. Nothing will be impossible for you" (Matthew 17:20). Did Jesus say "nothing?" Yes, that's what He promised. But faith is the key. Truly, success begins on your knees!

MAKING IT YOURS

1. After comparing an Old Testament (Nehemiah 8:1-9:3) and a New Testament (Acts 2:42, 46-47) service, what three elements of worship repeatedly stand out?

2. How might worship be defined as a triangle between God, ourselves and others?

3. How should God's Word be treated as "more than a vitamin" in your life?

4. Identify below three good reasons to read your Bible. Can you think of other reasons?
   - Romans 10:17
   - Ephesians 6:11-17
   - 1 Peter 2:2

5. God's Word has power, and prayed back to Him in faith, it unleashes miracles. Read 2 Chronicles 20:1-26. What overwhelming situation did King Jehoshaphat and Judah face?

6. What was the result of Judah's decision to trust and praise God in spite of their circumstances? (2 Chronicles 20:22-25)

7. Does faith-filled prayer mean I'm guaranteed my request as long as I base my prayers on God's Word and express faith in God? Explain. (Refer to Isaiah 55:8-9)

8. Worship is relational, too. Sometimes worship

enriches fellowship with other believers. At other times, worship brings conviction to lost souls. Consider the worship experiences listed below. How did each experience impact the world around it?

- Ezra's service in Jerusalem (Nehemiah 8:12-17)
- The worship of the early Christians (Acts 2:42, 45-47)
- The worship of King Jehoshaphat and Judah (2 Chronicles 20:29-30)

Chapter Twelve

You've Only Just Begun

THE HARE AND THE TORTOISE stood poised behind the starting line. Both were confident of victory. The hare was depending on his tremendous speed, while the tortoise looked to his plodding persistence to win the day. In a moment the race began. The hare bounded ahead. But, thinking he could always outrun the tortoise in the end, he soon stopped to nap.

Meanwhile, the tortoise continued his perpetual, stiff-legged gait toward the finish line. Near the end, the hare awoke and tried to overtake the tortoise, but it was too late. The tortoise's perseverance had won the day (Moore, 1954, 126, 127).

This fable highlights a very important lesson: success is a process. So often we mistakenly think that success is some undefinable level that we eventually attain. Like the hare, we consider only the finish line. We think: *The end is in sight. I can hardly wait! I'm almost there!*

But where is *there*? So often we sprint ahead to achieve our goals, only to realize that the finish line has moved to the next horizon. It is a discouraging realization. We expected success to be an end. Instead, we discover it is just a beginning. Often, we retreat for awhile, only to periodically gather ourselves (like the hare) for another dash at victory. The result is that our lives are lived in a staccato of energized bursts interrupted by despondent pauses. And if we ever stop to ask ourselves why life is so disappointing, we often overlook the simplest answer: success is a process. Victory goes not to the fastest, but the one that is faithful.

Success: A Process Governed by God

Neither is the race of life a solo endeavor. Paul took comfort in this fact as he wrote to the Christians at Philippi. He said:

> Being confident of this, that he who began a good work in you will carry it on to completion until the day of Christ Jesus. (Philippians 1:6)

We aren't in the race of life alone. Christ is at work in each Christian, helping him or her toward success.

And not only is God present in our life, but it is He who does the work. He is the one who carries on His refining in our lives—not us. Philippians 2:13 says: "For it is God who works in you to will and to act according to his good purpose." Our part is to simply obey His leading.

What a relief these truths are! One day I was out running near our small town. The wet, gray clouds of western Washington seemed draped around my soul as well as across the sky. I felt a heavy sense of frustration, anger and failure in my role as a pastor's wife. Not unlike the little Dutch boy who plugged the hole in the dike only to watch a multitude of other leaks begin. For just as I seemed to improve one area in my life, another area gave way. In anguish of soul, I screamed inwardly, "God, I can't do this! I'm just not cut out to be a pastor's wife!"

Immediately I heard His voice speaking to my heart: "I know *you* can't. I never intended *you* to be sufficient for the task. But *I* am. Lean on *Me!*"

How much easier life became when I relinquished control to Jesus Christ. In faith I gave Him the right to direct my life in this new role. I promised to obey His leading, realizing I needed His enabling even for this. It is a commitment I find myself renewing daily, and each time I'm struck anew with the reality of Christ's empowerment. Truly running life's race tandem with Jesus Christ beats running solo.

But Paul wasn't the first of God's servants to learn of God's strategy for success. A prophet of Judah, who lived many years earlier, learned the same lesson from angels.

Failure Isn't the End

In 538 B.C. King Cyrus (founder of the Achae-menid Persian empire that succeeded the Babylonian empire) issued an edict allowing the Jews living in Babylonian exile to return to their ancestral homeland. Many Jews responded by returning to Jerusalem. Nehemiah received leave of the king and returned to oversee the reconstruction of the walls of Jerusalem. Ezra worked alongside

Nehemiah, rebuilding both Jerusalem and Judah's spiritual heritage. Haggai and Zechariah were called of God in 520 B.C. to give a message of hope and spiritual renewal to this nation in the midst of reformation (Tenney, [1975] 1976, 1:1054, 5:1042-1043).

Zechariah's message was based on a series of visions. In these visions Zechariah was instructed by angels. In the first he saw a man astride a red horse. Later it became clear that this figure was none other than Christ. Angels mounted on other horses in the background were busy doing Christ's bidding throughout the world. Eventually, an angel began interceding for wayward Judah:

> LORD Almighty, how long will you withhold mercy from Jerusalem and from the towns of Judah, which you have been angry with these seventy years? (Zechariah 1:12)

The response is a message of God's grace.

> Therefore, this is what the LORD says, "I will return to Jerusalem with mercy, and there my house will be rebuilt. And the measuring line will be stretched out over Jerusalem," declares the LORD Almighty. (1:16)

The message is clear: failure need not be the end. With God there is always a future and the chance to begin afresh. Judah had failed repeatedly to be faithful to God's calling. In tough love, God allowed their rebellion to take them away into captivity. But He never abandoned them. Neither will He abandon us.

I confess, I've failed to be the perfect pastor's wife by my own standards, and often by the standards of those looking on. And there certainly are days I fall short of being the wife, mother or Christian I ought to be. But no matter how total my failure, I've also discovered that God's love stands true. How else can we understand His statement about wayward Judah in Zechariah 2:8? Christ says, "For whoever touches you touches the apple of his eye." This is possessive, ardent love. The same love God has toward every Christian—every pastor's wife—no matter how faithful or disappointing.

The Reality of Spiritual Warfare

Zechariah also learned the reality of spiritual warfare. In chapter 3, Satan is on the scene accusing Joshua, the high priest. But Christ again intercedes:

> The LORD said to Satan, "The LORD rebuke you, Satan! . . . Is not this man a burning stick snatched from the fire?" (3:2)

We not only have a Lord who prays for us, but who also defends us. In Romans 8 Paul asks:

> Who will bring any charge against those whom God has chosen? It is God who justifies. Who is he that condemns? Christ Jesus, who died—more than that, who was raised to life—is at the right hand of God and is also interceding for us. (8:33-34)

We could never hire a better lawyer in our defense.

Our deliverance is sure, because Christ has already paid the penalty of sin. Just as Joshua the high priest is clothed in new spotless clothing, so each of us exchanges the filthy rags of our own sinfulness for the righteousness of God.

But Satan doesn't give up easily. Even if he can't steal our righteousness, his accusations can make our Christian experience miserable. It is not surprising that he showed up in Zechariah to accuse one Christ had already "snatched from the fire." And Satan will accuse and abuse us also, if we will let him.

Part of the process of success, then, is learning to do spiritual warfare. Impediments stand in the way of all great victories. We applaud the athlete who covers the final, painful miles of a marathon, or the player who overcomes injury to return again to the game. The same is true of the Christian experience. To live the Christian life as God desires, we must learn to stand against Satan. Paul gave us an example of spiritual warfare as he defended his own ministry. He wrote:

> The weapons we fight with are not the weapons of the world. On the contrary, they have divine power to demolish strongholds. We demolish arguments and every pretension that sets itself up against the knowledge of God, and we take captive every thought to make it obedient to Christ. (2 Corinthians 10:4-5)

We have a great Defender in Jesus Christ. No victory has ever been more certain. But we will never experience that deliverance, unless, in faith, we take the offense against Satan, claiming our every thought captive to Jesus Christ.

The Power of Faith

If life is a roller coaster of ups and downs—if the Christian experience involves spiritual warfare with unseen forces—how can we ever expect to succeed? Certainly Zechariah must have wondered the same thing as he faced God's call to challenge Judah spiritually and finish rebuilding the Temple. The assignment was clear, but how indeed could such a task be accomplished?

Faith is the key. As an angel told Zechariah: "This is the word of the LORD to Zerubbabel: 'Not by might, nor by power, but by my spirit,' says the LORD Almighty" (Zechariah 4:6).

In chapter 8 God gave Zechariah a peek into the future. God shows him Jerusalem as a city of peace and prosperity where playing children will once again fill the streets. It seems an almost impossible transformation. The city was currently in disrepair, far from the glorious citadel pictured. God responded, "It may seem marvelous to the remnant of this people at that time, but will it seem marvelous to me?" (8:6). Obviously not—for nothing is impossible with God!

Bill and Tina had attended our church for some time when Tina finally gave her heart to Christ. Bill had also understood the gospel, but rejected Christ as Savior. Undaunted, my husband and I continued to pray for Bill's salvation.

Tina was baptized one Sunday, shortly before we were to move from our mountain pastorate. Afterwards, as we were visiting, I looked into Bill's gray eyes and said, "You know, someday that will be *you* up there getting baptized."

A wry grin spread across his face. "You think so, huh?" he responded.

"Yep!" I said gaily. "I'm praying for you."

Almost a year and a half later word reached us of Bill's conversion. We were thrilled, but hardly surprised. You see, nothing is impossible with God. Not the transformation of a ruined city, not the transformation of a ruined life. Where might and determination fail, the spirit of God succeeds. Christian success is the victory of faith.

He's at the Center

Where do you get your life? From where do you draw your sense of well being? Is it from your accomplishments, your ethnic heritage, your environment or relationships, that you draw your sense of worth? While all these things are important, there really is only one unshakable source for life: Jesus Christ.

The angels emphasized Christ's centrality over and over to Zechariah. In chapter 4 Christ is pictured as Zerubbabel (the current governor over Jerusalem). In Zechariah 4:7, obstacles as great as mountains become as nothing in His presence. Zechariah 4:9-10 says: "The hands of [Christ] have laid the foundation of this temple; his hands will also complete it. . . . Who despises the day of small things? Men will rejoice when they see the plumb line in the hand of [Christ]."

Christ is the source of accomplishment. He is at the center. As Matthew Henry wrote:

Herein [Zerubbabel] is a type of Christ, who is both the author and the finisher of our faith; and his being the author of it is an assurance to us that he will be the finisher, for, as for God, his work is perfect. (Henry n.d. 4:1419)

Who is at the center of your plans? Too often we ourselves are on the throne. We are all eager to have Christ as our Priest, but learning to love Him as our King takes time and experience. Indeed, it is a process begun at the moment of salvation that continues throughout our walk with Him. Yet the place of power is in His presence. In time, we learn of His ability to overcome any obstacle. In time, we find ourselves on our knees before Him rejoicing, "God bless it! God bless it!" (4:7b).

A Challenge to Live By

Scripture sums up the first section of Zechariah with a practical challenge that is applicable to our lives as well.

"Do not be afraid, but let your hands be strong. . . . These are the things you are to do: speak the truth to each other, and render true and sound judgment in your courts; do not plot evil against your neighbor, and do not love to swear falsely. I hate all this," declares the LORD. (8:13b, 16-17)

The first part of this challenge is: "Do not be afraid." It's a challenge repeated twice in this passage (8:13b and 8:15b). The opposite of fear is faith. God wants us to focus on Him and stand firm in our faith.

One evening following Jesus' resurrection, the disciples were meeting timidly behind locked doors when all of a sudden Jesus was in their midst. "Peace be with you!" Jesus said. Then He addressed the disciple most noted for his doubt—Thomas. He said, "Put your finger here; see my hands. Reach out your hand and put it into my side. Stop doubting and believe" (John 20:27). Thomas didn't need to touch. Instead, he cried out "My Lord and my God!" (20:28).

What doubts and fear assail you? You serve a Christ who has grasped victory from death itself! To each of us daily Christ holds out His scarred hands and challenges, "Stop doubting and believe." We need to believe Him for our own eternal salvation, but we need equally to believe Him for the challenges of every day. The Bible tells us that Jesus could do few miracles in His home town of Nazareth because of their lack of faith (Mark 6:5-6). I wonder, does Jesus often find a "Nazareth" in our hearts and turn away saddened that He is trusted to do so little. God help us!

The second part of Zechariah's challenge is a plea for faithfulness. Again, so we don't miss it, the challenge is repeated twice: "Let your hands be strong" (Zechariah 8:9, 13). The message is to keep on keeping on. Don't give up! Don't quit! Finish all that God has called you to—be faithful.

Faithfulness is easier said than done. Carol and I were the only two distance runners on our college women's track team. Accordingly we did our workout together almost daily. And although Carol was a tough competitor, she was also part coach at heart. Carol was always encouraging me to hang in there and keep going. One day she decided we should do an especially long workout that included running to the top of a steep bluff. At first I did fine, but before long the steep grade and long miles began to take their toll. Finally I suggested we stop. Instead of sympathy, Carol gave me a lecture on winning I've never forgotten. "Never stop running, Cheryl; no matter what," she said. "It's always too hard to get started again. And besides, running, no matter how slow, is still faster than walking."

We are all tempted to give up when life gets hard, aren't we? But that's when God wants us to look to Him in faith and hang in there. Anyone can quit. It takes faithfulness to be successful. In fact, success with God is simply faithful obedience.

A commitment to lordship might summarize the last part of Zechariah's challenge. In Zechariah 8:16–17 we are given a list of the type of behavior that does and doesn't honor God. We can't be a success in God's eyes if we aren't committed to living as He directs. Faith and true grit only have merit when they are focused on Christ. He is to be our all more and more each day.

There's More to Come!

When we have this challenge operating in our lives, God is free to work in miraculous ways. Zechariah 8 ends with a future description of Jerusalem. In that day it will be a city of incredible spiritual beauty drawing people from all around the world. Zechariah 8:23 says: "In those days ten men from all languages and nations will take firm hold of one Jew by the hem of his robe and say, 'Let us go with you, because we have heard that God is with you.' "

What a change from the shamed nation that suffered 70 years in exile because they could not remain faithful to God. Who would have thought that they will one day point the nations to Him? But this is the kind of change God can make. It is a change He makes not only in nations, but in the hearts of individuals as well. He wants to do such a work in your life. He wants to make you His beacon, shining triumphantly in a darkened world. Will you let Him? If you will, you've only just begun a great adventure destined to succeed.

MAKING IT YOURS

1. How can success be considered a process, rather than simply reaching a goal?

2. Would you define biblical success as a solo or team effort? Why? (Philippians 1:6; 2:13)

3. How do God's gracious dealings with Judah illustrate His desire to transform our failures as well? (Zechariah 1:12-17)

4. Spiritual warfare is one of the Christian's greatest barriers to success. The good news is that our victory is assured in Jesus Christ. It is our part that is the variable between success and failure. What can we do to realize this victory as we face daily temptations?

5. How should the amazing promise of Matthew 17:20 influence your perspective on failure and success?

6. What does it mean to "get your life" from Christ? (John 15:1-7; Colossians 3:3)

7. What is Zechariah's practical three-part challenge regarding success and failure?
   • Zechariah 8:13, 15
   • Zechariah 8:9, 13
   • Zechariah 8:16-17

Bibliography

Andersen, Hans Christian. *The Ugly Duckling*. New York: MacMillan, 1955.

Augsburger, David. *The Freedom of Forgiveness 70 x 7*. Chicago: Moody Press, 1970.

Backus, William and Marie Chapian. *Telling Yourself the Truth*. Minneapolis: Bethany House Publishers, 1980.

Briggs, Dorothy C. *Your Child's Self Esteem: The Key To Life*. Garden City: Doubleday & Co., 1970.

Briscoe, Jill. *By Hook or by Crook*. Waco, TX: Word Books Publishing, 1987.

Dobson, James. [1974] *Hide or Seek*. Old Tappan, NJ: Fleming H. Revell Co, 1979.

Jensen, Irving. *Jeremiah and Lamentations*. Chicago: Moody Press, 1966.

Lerner, Harriet Goldhor. *The Dance of Intimacy: A Woman's Guide to Courageous Acts of Change in Key Relationships*. New York: Harper & Row Publishers, 1989.

Lockyer Sr., Herbert., ed. *Nelson's Illustrated Bible Dictionary.* Nashville: Thomas Nelson Inc., Publishers, 1986.

Lutzer, Erwin. *FAILURE: The Back Door to Success.* Chicago: Moody Press, 1975.

Matthew Henry's Commentary On The Whole Bible. 6 vols. Old Tappan, NJ: Fleming H. Revell Co., n.d.

Moore, Marianne. [1952] *The Fables of La Fontaine.* New York: The Viking Press, 1954.

New Testament and Wycliffe Bible Commentary. 4th ed. New York: Iversen-Norman Assoc., 1971.

Statistical Abstract of the United States 1990. U.S. Dept. of Commerce. 110th annual ed. "Death Rates, By Cause—States: 1986" (Source: U.S. National Center for Health Statistics, Vital Statistics of the United States, annual).

Tenney, Merrill C. [1975] *The Zondervan Pictorial Encyclopedia of the Bible.* 5 vols. Grand Rapids: Zondervan, 1976.

Twain, Mark. *The Prince and the Pauper.* Garden City: Junior Deluxe Editions, 1954.

Webster's New Collegiate Dictionary. Springfield, MA: G & C Merriam Co., 1974.

Wright, H. Norman. *Training Christians to Counsel.* Eugene, OR: Harvest House Publishers, 1983.